D0839730

HUMAN DIGNITY & HUMAN NUMBERS

HUMAN DIGNITY & HUMAN NUMBERS

James V. Schall, S.J.

alba house A DIVISION OF THE SOCIETY OF ST. PAUL
STATEN ISLAND, NEW YORK 10314

Nihil Obstat
Daniel V. Flynn, J.C.D.
Censor Librorum

Imprimatur
Joseph P. O'Brien, S.T.D.
Vicar General, Archdiocese of New York
May 18, 1971

The nihil obstat and imprimatur are official declarations that a book or pamphlet is free of doctrinal or moral error. No implication is contained therein that those who have granted the nihil obstat and imprimatur agree with the contents, opinions or statements expressed.

ISBN: 0-8189-0217-5

Library of Congress Catalog Card Number: 70-169143

Designed, printed and bound in the U.S.A. by the Pauline Fathers and Brothers of the Society of St. Paul, 2187 Victory Blvd., Staten Island, N.Y. 10314 as part of their communications apostolate.

HN
16.
.S3

PREFACE

Throughout the world today, there is great and necessary concern
about population and environmental questions. There is,
no doubt, reason for this.

However, as I have studied and reflected about the
phenomenon as it is now being presented in the public forum, I have become increasingly disturbed by the
evident and glaring contrasts and exaggerations I have
found being presented as "truth" even in the most scholarly circles. Why was it, I began to ask myself, that such diverse
opinions could be held among so many evidently qualified thinkers?

The result of pursuing this problem is this book. The position
I take here goes contrary to much of the mood of the times.
This cannot be helped. That is where I believe the evidence and
the sensibility goes.

For this reason, I have thought it well, indeed necessary to
document thoroughly from a wide variety of sources what I have

to say. Many will find this annoying, as I do sometimes myself.

Nonetheless, the main point I wish to make is that this is not an open and shut case by any means. There are problems so serious connected with population and environmental control proposals that we can only ignore them at our peril.

Consequently, I have sought here to trace and state objectively the origins and implications of these recent proposals. I have also tried to show that there is considerable counter-evidence — evidence not nearly well enough known — to most of the population and environmental theories. It is there, if anyone is willing to pursue it.

I should hope that the spirit of what I have to say is calm and rational enough. In this book, I am really more concerned with philosophic and intellectual questions than counter-action for I believe that the main struggle is really in the realm of ideas. Yet, I have no illusions about the political and human consequences of continuing to follow so many present theories which are contrary to our traditions, to the best interests and dignities of the ordinary man.

Thus I hope here to spell out such dangerous trends in some orderly fashion. My feeling is that facts and theories are very much more related in this area than we are often given to suspect. Consequently, I hope that both my theory about man and the facts I believe support it are clearly and forcefully argued.

I recognize, moreover, that my position is, in effect, a "minority" one in today's climate of opinion. However, I believe it is the right one and that it is absolutely necessary for someone to argue it. I am indeed, amazed, yes, appalled about the lack of critical thinking about population and environment in traditional Christian and liberal sources. Paradoxically, only a few beknighted engineers and scientists seem to be upholding the human tradition in the modern world. I believe this neglect to be both intellectually unnecessary and morally disastrous if my analysis is anywhere near the truth.

The position I take and the argument I follow, furthermore, are not primarily, or even mainly religious ones, even though I will seem to many quick readers to be simply following a traditional line. This is not the case. The only really surprising point I wish to make in respect to religion is this: why is it that traditional religious concepts about human dignity and growth, about human sexuality and intelligence turn out to be the very ones that modern science and technology need to guide themselves through their own inventions and their relation with the earth and man? This seems somehow uncanny to me, even at times frightening.

Nevertheless, I do think there is a common good that could conceivably reunite all the various forces so much at loggerheads today over population and nature. This good lies in the reality of man's unique destiny and in the nature of this planet. Our thinking in this field has been, on all sides, much too loose and inadequate to come effectively to a newer, more solid position.

Man's destiny on this earth has only begun. I believe that we can and must pursue it, — but pursue it as the funny, fallible, mortal creatures we are. Population and environmental theory, I greatly suspect, is beginning to deny, if it is not more careful than it has been, both the destiny and the reality of the man who is to pursue it. We must, ultimately, keep man to be man, if we are to keep our nature and that of the world we have been given.

CONTENTS

INTRODUCTION

TOO MANY CONTRADICTIONS

To write anything at all about the population problem must always be, confessedly, somewhat rash. Probably no group of experts in the modern world has been so consistently proved wrong by subsequent events as "population" forecasters. From Malthus right up to the present "Green Revolution," something unforeseen always seemed to turn up which unexpectedly threw out of order even the most balanced projections of future population growth or decline. In retrospect, we are told, an unanticipated design revolution, a baby boom, a crop failure, bad weather, good weather, a vaccine, DDT, plant diseases occurred to throw the "scientific" forecast out of kilter.[1] We cannot, of course,

1. Cf. Ralph Thomlinson, *Population Dynamics,* New York, Random House, 1965, pp. 47-72; Michel Cépède and others, *Population and Food,*

use this kind of historical record to prove that all forecasts must necessarily be invalid. Yet, a certain healthy caution and hesitation are definitely in order when dealing with the question of population statistics.

But there is a further risk. To write about population from the viewpoint of someone who is, in many ways, rather impressed with the values of the more traditional Christian and humanistic concepts on this vexing subject must seem doubly rash, if not down-right absurd. Yet, there is a case to be made for them. And what is even more surprising is that this case arises mostly from scientific grounds themselves. Admittedly, the older voice seems to be almost silenced in today's public discussion, even for those who might be most expected to argue for it. Almost the only way it appears in the public forum is as something to be "against." And this is tragically unfortunate.

We must, then, be *free* enough intellectually to consider at least the possibility that there is something essential involved in the more historic view that merits present attention. Too many

---

New York, Sheed and Ward, 1964, pp. 37-67; Dennis Wrong, *Population and Society,* New York, Random House, 1966, pp. 1-24. "There is also the possibility that they could be wrong about the trends themselves. Population, for example. The past track record of the experts has been miserable. Back in the thirties, the best informed opinion was that the then low birth rate would continue and that this country probably would never have more than 150 million people. Population decline was a problem many thoughtful people worried about, and one of the arguments then advanced for new planned communities was that they would furnish environment that would stimulate more child breeding.

But the birth rate increased. Experts thought this might be temporary. In 1945 they predicted that the birth rate might rise for a few years as the soldiers came home but it would then drop back. The birth rate rose, and kept on rising for fifteen years.

It is this momentum that has been built into most current projections. But the momentum may already be spent. Since 1957, the birth rate has been going down, not up. The decline may be reversed, of course. But it may not. It may even accelerate. In bracing ourselves to meet a huge population surge, we may have set in motion some subtle but powerful counterforce." William H. Whyte, *The Last Landscape,* Doubleday Anchor, 1970, pp. 169-70.

are simply writing off the question as not worthy of further serious thought. Very few are free enough any more philosophically to take another, more profound look at the problem of population. No subject seems to encourage a higher factor of passion and prejudice. This itself should lead us to suspect a crucial issue is involved which touches the essence of man. Thus, there is more of a problem of intellectual freedom involved here than is commonly realized. The problem, in essence, lies rather more here than in the area of "facts" as such.

Nevertheless, the real reasons which indicate that there is something more to the essentials of Christian tradition than meets the eye do not primarily arise from the exigencies of theology. Indeed, whenever the question is studied from a purely "theological" point of view, if there is such a thing, it often appears that the liberal criticism of the traditional position is correct.[2] A significant number of theologians would argue for a radical change in the traditional positions about population to come into conformity with the predominant positions found in the secular writers on this subject.

Nevertheless, in the long run, what suggests that the theories of population and its control are of a theoretical and metaphysical nature are precisely the most articulate and dogmatic advocates of universal and obligatory birth and population control. Paul VI alone, to be sure, could probably never convince us of the enormous dangers to humanity in this area. But Julian Huxley, William Vogt, Paul Ehrlich, Sir Charles Galton Darwin, Garret Hardin, Robert Rienow, and Bertrand Russell leave little room for rational doubt because what they propose is nothing less than a complete overturning of the values that humanity once

---

2. A representative essay of this sort would be, V. R. Gorospe, "The Church and Regulation of Birth," *Philippine Studies,* July, 1969, pp. 566-87; cf. also J. Goffinet, "Pour une morale de situation chrétienne," *Revue Ecclésiastique de Liège,* #1, 1963, pp. 3-29; Paul Anciaux, "Ethical Aspects of Demographic Policy," *World Justice,* Spring 1963, pp. 5-20; Charles Curran, *Contemporary Moral Theology,* Fides, 1970.

believed essential for its dignity and well-being. Indeed, had Paul VI somehow approved population control as it is now being proposed, we would have had to disagree with him on the grounds that we had read Joshua Lederberg, Gore Vidal, Kenneth Boulding, and the Japanese abortion statistics. As even Christian theologians are now moving toward a theoretical acceptance of abortion as a legitimate possibility and as professional population critics are more and more despairing over the prospects of family planning by voluntary or artificial means, it becomes evident that, however we choose to argue, human life is literally what is at issue.[3]

The approach of this population analysis is, in part, from that of political theory. It is a fascinating background from which to approach it as it is evident that population questions are now becoming ever more "political." Population writers are, as a rule, highly innocent with regard to the history of political thought and the significance of man's perennial struggle with totalitarian and authoritarian governments. They are also too often, as Alexander B. Adams has noted, naive about practical politics, though this has changed very rapidly in the past few years.[4]

In any case, political thought possesses an integrated wholeness about it which can be underscored from two major aspects:

1) The progressive expansion of human rights and dignities is a progress and, more importantly, a secular and religious obli-

3. Cf. Francis Simons, "The Catholic Church and the New Morality," *Cross Currents,* Fall 1966, pp. 438ff.; Thomas Wassmer, "Questions About Questions," *The Commonweal,* 30 June 1967, pp. 416-18; Charles H. Bayer, "Confessions of an Abortion Counselor," *Christian Century,* 20 May 1970, 624-26; James E. Krause, "Is Abortion Absolutely Prohibited?" *Continuum,* Autumn 1968. Cf. the analyses of the various aspects of this discussion in Enda McDonagh, "Ethical Problem of Abortion," *Irish Theological Quarterly,* 35 (1968), 268-97; G. Grisez, "Abortion and the Catholic Faith," *American Ecclesiastical Review,* August 1968, pp. 96-115; and R. Springer, "Notes on Moral Theology," *Theological Studies,* September 1970, pp. 492-507.

4. Cf. Alexander B. Adams, *The Eleventh Hour,* New York, G. P. Putnam's Sons, pp. 324-48.

gation.[5] This secular obligation itself has theological implications and dimensions so that, as we shall see, a change in the concept of man will and is involving a change in theology.[6] But we must also render to Caesar, that is, the population problem has by right its own political context.

2) Politics belongs to the world of real men. Politics, therefore, must also include not merely the element of human idealism, but also a realism that must come to terms with and control the dire consequences of man's sins and crimes against himself. It is not moral or even possible for politicians to withdraw from social realities in the name of moral purity or compassion if they thereby leave the field open to more sinister forces. Such an attitude of rejection of the real problems in the name of keeping moral innocence has always in the past increased, not decreased

5. Cf. the author's *Redeeming the Time*, New York, Sheed and Ward, 1968, Chapter II.

6. Cf. A. Vergote, "The Church in Tomorrow's Society," *Catholic Mind*, December 1970, pp. 42-51.

Russell Kirk notes a very critical aspect of this relationship:

"In our age, probably more than in most eras, there are many persons in rebellion against the wisdom of our ancestors. As such, the spiritual and intellectual patrimony of our civilization seems a burden, rather than a foundation . . . . So far as our Christian heritage is concerned, there is not the slightest danger that Christianity may cease to be popular in America. The peril, rather, is that the Christian religion may become altogether too popular for its own good. Tocqueville remarked upon the tendency of the American democracy to refashion religion on a democratic pattern, to abolish all intermediary power between God and man, and to emphasize the social aspects of religious faith at the expense of the supernatural . . . .

Yet, the quality of that religious faith is another matter. The American Protestant clergy — and, to a lesser extent, even the Roman Catholic clergy — tend markedly toward what is called the 'social gospel,' the sentimental and humanitarian application of religious doctrines to the reform of mundane society at the expense of supernatural elements in religion and the personal element in morality. There also exists a tendency toward making the Church into a club and a means of communal self-gratulation. Christian hope and Christian resignation both suffer under this domination of materialism and democracy in the Church." "Roots of Our Civilization," *Phalanx*, Spring 1967, p. 13.

the amount of suffering and chaos among men. There is a kind of political angelism towards the immoralities of public life — an attitude today found, curiously enough, more on the left than on the right — which is difficult to justify.[7] We can never be unconscious of the essential conflict between the greater and the lesser evils that in fact occurs in political life.

This double commitment of political theory leaves unsettling paradoxes that must be recognized. We can, for example, thoroughly hate abortion in all its aspects because it is, in its overall context, the great evil of modern times and the moral Achilles' heel of our civilization. Yet, politicians have to control this phenomenon when it happens in their societies. The political action to contain and regulate such a thing as abortion seems ethical if it appears to be a wise political judgment. Yet, in itself, it is still a moral evil. Thus, an optimism that does not correspond with the realities of men who actually exist is the most subtle form of anti-humanism.

Consequently, when we read, for example, such earnest and not unrepresentative pleading of a young university graduate, a certain skepticism seems in order:

> With us (feminine graduates of 1969) too, goes an absolute commitment to moral justice, racial equality, and personal freedom that we have learned here (at Berkeley). We shall teach love, not hate, compassion, not cruelty, honesty not hypocrisy; we shall teach that what is in man's heart is more important than the color of his skin; we shall teach that the commandment "Thou Shalt Not Kill" is sacred, regardless of war, or riot, or criminal justice. We shall not only talk, we shall act . . . .[8]

7. Cf. the author's "Ethics and International Affairs," *World Justice,* #4, 1965, pp. 462-75; "Caesar As God," *The Commonweal,* 6 February 1970, pp. 505-10.

8. Anne Roberts, "Woman, 1969 — Exit into Subtle Revolution," *The Daily Californian,* Berkeley, 20 June 1969.

On the surface, this seems like exalted idealism. But there is a certain fierceness about it that transcends human reality. Real men are going to have such aberrations somehow among them. And we must live with their failures. This absoluteness is the perennial background to the terror, for it is not talking about the human situation of real men. Too, this is believed to be a very new doctrine. We would really like to believe it is new and that humanity has had no experience with the existential consequence of this pure theory.

But it is not so new or so innocent. Such an affirmation that this is new could only come from a college generation so involved in the "now" of its four or five years in the university that it never had time to know and ponder the "yesterday," the what has gone before. Why is it, history forces us to ask, that such pure idealism always seems to have been the prelude to some kind of repression?[9]

This seemingly new doctrine is very much like old gnosticism. We must be slow to accept this kind of innocence elevated to a metaphysical theory in which the elect have elected themselves, in which they have no tears for their own sins and finiteness, in which social sins are incorporated in the organization of someone else. Human life does need protection. There are criminals. Individuals and peoples are attacked. It would be nice if a Hitler could not possibly have existed, perhaps, but such is not the kind of world we are in. The best way to multiply evil is to accept such a neognostic theory that has no place for evil's reality except as an affirmation that it belongs to some other world, that nothing need to be done about it because it does not exist for the new, pure man who is to have, supposedly, no "hate," no "cruelty," no "hypocrisy." Such new men do not and cannot exist and still be men.

To deny the need to recognize and to do something about the

9. Cf. Philip K. Kurland, "The New American University," *Vital Speeches*, 1 March 1970, pp. 314-17.

wielders of what must be called "evil" or corruption is tanta-
mount to denying the reality of freedom. Freedom is never more
in jeopardy than when the evil is seen as something that need not
be confronted. "The good that can be derived from evil,"
Berdyaev wrote in his classic study of Dostoevsky,

> is attained only by way of suffering and repudiation of evil.
> Dostoevsky believed firmly in the redemptive and regenerative
> power of suffering: life is the expiation of sin by suffering.
> Freedom has opened the path of evil to man, it is proof of
> freedom, and man must pay the price. The price is suffering,
> and by it the freedom that has been spoiled and turned into
> its contrary is reborn and given back to man.[10]

The suffering and the agony are the signs and the consequences
of the freedom. Whenever we sense that a philosophy or intellectual
mood is really based upon the belief that these realities of suffering
and freedom can be removed completely from man, or that evil
is merely the consequence of social forms or genetic formation,
then we are very near to the denial of freedom itself, near to
the denial of the man we know from experience and history.
This is really the underlying question of modern times and nowhere is this more true than in the theory and practice that sur-
rounds the modern population question.

Nevertheless, the immediate interest in population from a
theoretical point of view comes from quite a diverse source, from
a strange, nagging curiosity caused by examining the contemporary
literature on the subject. We must, obviously, grant the value and
need of population studies. Nor is there much doubt that a
serious problem of some kind does exist for mankind in this area.
Yet, there persists the curiosity. After reading many divergent yet
representative studies of population problems, there is no escaping

10. Nicholas Berdyaev, *Dostoevsky,* New York, Living Age Books, 1966,
p. 95.

the fact that fundamental, radical inconsistencies are somehow present in the structure of the whole topic.[11]

The intrinsic contradictions in current population analyses are an intellectually chastening and yet stimulating experience. For there is no escaping the glaring fact that there are just too many "competent" discrepancies. This is another way of saying that no one can escape the hard task of formulating what he stands for, of determining where he draws the human line in discussing population. The subject itself forces the issues. What is of absolute certainty is that the line of what is human must be drawn somehow both morally and politically if we are to retain human dignity. And this task is a philosophical and theological act that sets down the structure of the kind of man who is to survive and grow in the centuries to come.

In this context, then, what are we to make of the contradictions in the contrasting affirmations of Mr. Julian Huxley and Mr. Buckminster Fuller? For Huxley,

. . . the world's demographic situation is becoming impossible. Man, in person of the present generation of human beings, is

11. Read, for example, the following essays in sequence:
    1) Julian Huxley, "The World Population Problem," *The Human Crisis*, Seattle, University of Washington Press, 1963, pp. 43-88.
    2) R. Buckminster Fuller, "Man With a Chronofile," *The Saturday Review*, April 1, 1967, pp. 14-18.
    3) Joshua Lederberg, "Experimental Genetics and Human Evolution," *The Bulletin of the Atomic Scientists*, October 1966.
    4) Colin Clark, "Do Population and Freedom Go Together?" *Fortune*, December 1960.
    5) Paul Erhlich, *The Population Bomb*, New York, Ballantine, 1969.
    6) Karl Brandt, "The Population Dilemma," *Vital Speeches*, 1963, pp. 629-31.
    7) Richard N. Gardner, "The Quality of Life," *Vital Speeches*, 15 May 1970, pp. 466-70.
    8) Ben Wattenberg, "Overpopulation as a Crisis Issue: The Nonsense Explosion," *The New Republic*, April 4 & 11, 1970, pp. 18-23.

laying a burden on his own future. He is condemning his children's children to increased misery; he is making it harder to improve the general lot of mankind; he is making it more difficult to build a united world free of frustration and greed. More and more human beings will be competing for less and less, or at any rate, will have to be content with a lesser cut of the world's cake. . . .[12]

For Fuller, on the other hand,

Fortunately, population explosion is only the momentary social hysteria's cocktail conversation game. Real population crisis is extremely remote. There is enough room indoors in New York City for the whole of 1963's world population to enter, with enough room inside for all hands to dance the twist in average night club proximity . . . .[13]

This would suggest, therefore, that serious divergencies exist about the "facts" — so much so that we must recognize how much "the facts of population" are determined by prior commitments and philosophical suppositions, or lack of them.

This conclusion is not a skeptical one. There is a relation between sane philosophy and sensible facts. The one somehow seems to require the other. Anything that touches the basic human mystery will almost necessarily leave arguments and conclusions that can seem to support conflicting views about the meaning of man. Man is problematic even about himself. And the faith is not to be forced, nor is its lack. This is the one absolute rule that governs reality, scientific and popular.

In this sense, then, what is most disturbing about the question of population is not the nature of the "facts." Rather it is the phenomenon of watching apparently sincere, committed, in-

12. Huxley, p. 79.
13. R. Buckminster Fuller, "Prime Design," in *Beyond Left and Right,* ed. R. Kostelanetz, New York, Morrow, 1968, p. 363.

telligent human beings give up, in the almost holy name of population, some of the essential values of humanity as we have known them. Consequently, it is cause for considerable reflection when we read someone so sensible and intelligent as Professor Kenneth Boulding calmly proposing, in the name of population, something that strikes at the very heart of humanity:

> I think in all seriousness, however, that a system of marketable licenses to have children is the only one which will combine the minimum of social control necessary to the solution of this problem with the maximum of individual liberty and ethical choice. Each girl on approaching maturity would be presented with a certificate which will entitle its owner to have, say, 2.2 children, or whatever number would ensure a reproduction rate of one.[14]

This and the vast array of similar alternative proposals such as those outlined by Professor Berelson cannot but startle any sensitive commitment and belief in historical man.[15]

Professor Boulding himself admits that he is hesitant about such a "logical" result of his reasoning. But he sees no way out. So he is willing to give up the human rights that might be involved in order to solve what seems to him to be the greater law. In short, what we are told is that there is no longer to be a

14. Kenneth Boulding, *The Meaning of the Twentieth Century*, New York, Harper, Row, Inc., 1964, p. 135.
15. Cf. Bernard Berelson, "Beyond Family Planning," *Studies in Family Planning*, February 1969; J. Mayone Stycos, "Effective Implementation of Fertility Control Programs," in *Readings on Population*, ed. D. Heer, Englewood Cliffs, N. J., Prentice-Hall, 1968, pp. 218-29; Linda Witt, "The Male Contraceptive: The Bitter Pill," *Today's Health*, June 1970, pp. 17-19; "Patterns of Human Reproduction," *WHO Chronicle*, March 1970, pp. 112-14; Frank W. Notestein, Dudley Kirk and Sheldon Segal, "The Problem of Population Control," in *The Population Dilemma*, ed. P. Hauser, Englewood Cliffs, N. J., Spectrum, 1969, pp. 139-67; V. Petrow, "Current Aspects of Fertility Control," *Chemistry in Britain*, 4 April 1970, pp. 167-71. Cf. also the author's "Christian Political Approaches to Population Problems," *World Justice*, March 1967, pp. 301-23.

"higher law" except the exigencies of population control. What is really at issue, then, is a faith, not merely a faith in a God who made man to be of a certain structure or capacity, but rather a faith in man and his intelligence to live this human heritage without at the same time attacking its very essentials.

The smoothness and ease with which the public opinion of the world, and of the United States in particular, has been almost panicked about pollution and population must be one of the all-time fascinating studies in the history of propaganda. And what is particularly interesting about this panic atmosphere is the anti-scientific and anti-technological undertone behind it all. "The moment calls for a redirection of technology, not an intensification of it. . . . There is no such direction of technology possible, and little rehabilitation of our habitat, until we shift our ground on what beliefs we as a people hold." [16] This alone should make us wonder about it.

The Italian scientific review *Sapere* has noted in a perceptive editorial the irony of such a trend. In the Sixties, science was seen in the beginning to be an essential aspect of economic and cultural development so that the politicians finally were convinced that they should foster and promote it.

16. Robert Rienow and Leona Train Rienow, "The Age of Eternal Twilight," *Audubon*, July 1970, p. 8.

"*Homo faber* has a staunch faith in the future. Tomorrow he will move mountains, change the course of rivers, gather harvests in the desert, go to the moon. And a terribly utilitarian concept has taken possession of us. We are interested only in what can be used now.

This confidence in our technical ability leads us to destroy everything that is still wild and to convert all men to the cult of the machine. Our ambition is to persuade pygmies, Papuans and Indians of the Amazon, to adopt 'Western Civilization,' since we believe that the only pattern for life is that laid down by the inhabitants of Chicago, London or Paris. We have firm faith in technical progress and in the need for making the whole world think as we do . . . .

But suppose man was mistaken in putting so much faith in his new types. The civilization we are now creating can only lead man to ruin." Jean Dorst, *Before Nature Dies*, trans. C. D. Sherman, Boston, Houghton, Mifflin, 1970, p. 327.

But approximately after 1965, with an ever-increasing frequency, voices arose which doubted the illuminist thesis that the expansion of knowledge could only benefit mankind. They asked if the well-being of man really depended on his physical well-being. They accused the consumption society, itself a direct inheritor of the myth of progress, of gradually and inescapably destroying the natural environment of man. They cast anathemas at the irresponsibility of the makers of nuclear arms.

Such theses are sustained, furthermore, with petulance among some youth movements which greet gladly the destruction of the system which has brought this about and especially its principal determinant, science. The man in the street and the politician who had accepted with reluctance in the beginning the cause of scientific and technological progress remain perplexed before the critics of every age group and are incertain about which way to go.[17]

The relation of science to our civilization is more and more being ignored because it is essential to destroy the hopes produced by science to prove the dire theses about the blackness of our future.[18]

17. "É Davvero Nefasta La Scienza?" *Sapere,* January 1970, p. 3.
"Our challenge, as I see it, is to find a way to rebalance the scales between the growing power of scientific knowledge and the continuing weakness of man. Just as man has the capacity to create knowledge, so he has the capacity to control its use .... We must not allow the growing public concern about research and technology to outrun reason and knowledge. The dangers of this are already apparent in the case of insecticides where public outcry against DDT may be drowning out the voices of science and common sense. Public opinion is overtaking and may swamp us. If we do not respond by providing leadership, we may soon awaken to find not only that technology has been crudely shackled, but that fundamental scientific inquiry itself is in jeopardy." Max Tishler, "To Awaken the Virtue of a Careless Age" (Priestly Award Address, American Chemical Society), *Chemical and Engineering News,* 9 March 1970, pp. 81-82.
18. Cf. Philip Handler, President of the US National Academy of Sciences, "Sombre Greeting from Abroad," *Nature,* 27 December 1969, p. 1250. Cf. also regarding the growing anti-intellectual environment in

The panic and the bleakness are almost all current articles of faith. "The media which can bang pots and ring bells for the most insignificant causes," Nicholas von Hoffman, has prophesied,

> has yet to put on its first anti-baby campaign. Where are the TV spots giving people a realistic assessment of what kind of a life that baby's going to live? Where are the billboards proclaiming fast-breeding animals are pests? Why are we still making over multi-children mothers and having Father of the Year contests? . . . . The last moment may come before the planet can no longer sustain human life; it may come when the press of too many crazy people killing and cutting each other destroys our human communities. That's what some social scientists believe.[19]

Thus, we are told that there is little hope, that we must act, now, that nothing remains if we do not.[20]

What is surprising is how few voices there really are who see the totalitarian implications in this kind of reasoning.[21] Not only is there little challenging of such "facts" that are presented to prove that there is no hope, but there is little clear comprehension of the meaning of the depth or direction of the panic. Stewart Alsop is one of the few who clearly tells us what the alternative is and recognizes that it may well be more dangerous than population growth.

the universities, the author's "The University, Revolution and Freedom," *Studies*, Summer 1969, pp. 115-26.

19. Nicholas von Hoffman, "Baby Boom Goes Whimper," *The Washington Post*, 16 January 1970. It might also be interesting to note the movie, *No Blade of Grass* which attempts to set the ecological-population theme to film. Alas, it may well be the worst movie ever made.

20. A good collection which attempts to substantiate this attitude would be *The Environmental Handbook*, prepared for the First National Environmental Teach-In, ed. G. de Bell, New York, Ballantine, 1970.

21. One of the few exceptions is the essay of Ben Wattenburg cited in Footnote 11, #8.

Or take the pollution issue, which the President has embraced with such enthusiasm. Pollution, after all, is caused by people. . . . Given the present population-growth rate, the best that can be done is to slow down the process of pollution. Actually to reverse the process would require zero population growth or close to it. It is most unlikely that Mr. Nixon, or any other politician who wishes to remain in public office in this democracy, is going seriously to propose anything of the sort . . . .

(If growth and unrest continue) then there will be a great national temptation to resort to authoritarian measures to deal with those problems which seem otherwise so insoluble. . . . At least the mysterious American disease does not appear to be lethal, and it is worth bearing in mind that an authoritarian cure can be much worse than a democratic disease.[22]

What we lack today is an almost total neglect on the part of the scholarly community to analyze the "authoritarian cure" as it is being proposed in the population field. Mr. Alsop is surely right in his warning.

Perhaps the ease with which such totalitarian and authoritarian proposals are coming forward today in the academic and public opinion spheres represents one of the greatest weaknesses in mankind's intellectual climate. Karl Brandt sees this to be the real issue. And it casts a grim shadow over everything written and proposed in the contemporary world about population. "Unless we are willing to abandon the values on which freedom and respect for human dignity stand or fall," Professor Brandt observed,

we must recognize that the real issues of our topic are neither essentially biological or medical ones — but belong in the realm of the pursuit of happiness of human beings living in

22. Stewart Alsop, "The Mysterious American Disease," *Newsweek*, 9 February 1970, p. 28.

organized social units. The problems . . . are of utter complexity — to all those among us who have respect for different
cultures, the right of self-determination of nations, the rights
of individuals and families to choose and make decisions
in their preference for life and work — within the frame of
law and order.[23]

It is the suspicion that the present state of population theory —
no matter how well intended — involves the lessening or destruction of man as we have received him from nature and history that
makes population studies more than statistics and economics,
makes them, in fact, something fusing into metaphysics and theology.[24]

   There is, then, some value and consequence in analyzing and
setting forth the various trends in population theory and practice
so that we can, if possible, draw from their logical consequences
in order that they may be clearly seen and understood. The approach of such an analysis must be quiet and contemplative.
Everyone, it must be acknowledged, is in some way anxious about

   23. Brandt, *Vital Speeches,* 1 August 1963, p. 629.
   24. It is noteworthy that professional population literature itself is
more and more admitting, as we shall point out in the next chapter, that
the questions are really political and metaphysical, not "scientific." The
rather startling comment of Rufus E. Miles is worth noting here: "The
question whether we have a population problem, therefore, is directly
related to the question whether we have a freedom problem. To the
extent that people are concerned about direct threats to and the slow
erosions of their freedom, they must seek genuine and controllable causes.
If they do, the logic of their analysis is almost certain to bring them
face to face with growing population as a major cause of the diminution
of human freedom. *Scientists may argue for a decade or a century over how
many people may theoretically be sustained on this planet and in this
nation, but the strength of human desires for personal and political freedom
and for mobility will determine the course of America's birth rate far
more than scientific analysis. The balance of this paper is based on the
unprovable proposition that we do, indeed, have a population problem.*"
"Whose Baby Is the Population Problem?" *Population Bulletin,* Vol. 26,
No. 1, February, 1970, p. 8. Italics added.

man. Much of what is said here, furthermore, goes contrary to popular and "scientific" beliefs in certain scholarly and public areas. But we must also be conscious of the fact that we are dealing here with choices and values. Human life has a quality of chance about it. It can be won or lost. And we are in danger of losing because we fail to think about what is really being proposed in the area of population.

Nevertheless, if humanity really does eventually lose, if it actually destroys its nature and history and habitat, it will do so not because it *must,* but because it *willed* to do so. There is nothing in theology or politics that allows us to think that the ultimate destruction or degradation, should it come from proposals in the population field, would result from anything less than a free, collective choice. And so if we are to avoid such a consequence, we must likewise make a free, cooperative choice about what we are. Mankind will only remain mankind if it chooses to do so. This is the nature of the time in which we live. It is also the dignity of the being that man is.

THE DRIFT OF POPULATION THEORY

1 Population is not primarily a question of numbers. Numbers, by themselves, are abstractions, more properly classified as mathematical constructs or tools. Human numbers must always be seen in function of the nature and dignity of the thing numbered, that is, of man. Human numbers, then, are relational, calculations proportioned to other likewise variable numbers and factors, figures that can never be grasped in their pure isolation as mere numbers. Any citation of human numbers in isolation from other numbers and rates of growth is, *ipso facto,* misleading.

No doubt, it is senseless to argue with mathematical projections. Carlo Cipolla, in a representative example, cites forecasts that are designed to illustrate graphically the meaning of population growth rates.[1] If world population augments at two per cent per year (or at any per cent, for that matter) and this rate (or any rate) remains constant over time, population will eventually and necessarily reach infinite figures, no matter with how many men the computation begins (two or two billion) or when (2,000,000 BC, 86 AD, or Yesterday Afternoon). It is absolutely and totally senseless to argue with such compound population arithmetic. Here, it is taken for granted that such statistics, as statistics, are valid. What is not taken for granted is that statistics can be considered to act in the same way as human beings.

Further, then, the necessity of some change in population growth rates as we have known them, especially during the post-World War II years, is obvious. As a matter of fact, projections of actual population growth rates have been revised sharply downward both in the United States and in the world in general in recent years. Ben Wattenberg, in his article, "Overpopulation as a Crisis Issue: The Nonsense Revolution," (*The New Republic,* April 4 & 11, 1970, p. 19), explains:

"This human plaint tells us what has been happening demographically in the United States in recent years. It has not been a population explosion, but a population redistribution. . . .

"But even the total increase in population—rural, city, and suburb—is misleading. The big gains in population occurred ten

1. "The population of an agricultural society is characterized by a normal rate of growth of 0.5 to 1.0 per cent per year. To give a meaning to this figure I can quote an exercise in astronomical arithmetic by P. C. Putnam: If the race had sprung from a couple living not long before agriculture was discovered — let us say 10,000 BC — and if its members had expanded at the rate of one per cent per year since then, the world population would form today a sphere of living flesh many thousand light years in diameter, and expanding with a radical velocity that, neglecting relativity, would be many times faster than light." Carlo M. Cipolla, *The Economic History of World Population,* Penguin, 1964, pp. 76-77. Similar mathematical exercises can be found in almost any contemporary discussion of population.

and fifteen years ago; today growth is much slower. Thus, in calendar year 1956, the U.S. population grew by 3.1 million, while in calendar year 1968 population went up by two million and in a nation with a larger population base.

"What has happened, simply, is that the baby-boom has ended."

Carl E. Taylor, in his article, "Population Trends in an Indian Village," (*Scientific American,* July, 1970, p. 106), states:

"There is reason for optimism about the demographic future of India. To be sure, most demographers are gloomy about India's population problems, and when I consider the over-all statistical projections, I tend to share their concern. Then I come back to our research base in the Punjab, in northwestern India, and feel the stirrings of social and economic development. I note the birth rates have begun to decline in the Punjab and at the scattered sites of demonstration projects in other parts of the country. I realize that recent progress has been dramatic, and then even the vastly accelerated program that is still essential begins to seem possible."

Population growth rates cannot remain mathematically stable. The issue, however, is over the how and the why, though the "how many" is also a more important figure than is generally realized. It seems clear that in this area we deal with problems that are not merely mathematical. Numbers, as such, finally force us to metaphysical and theological issues about the being and destiny of man and nature.

Population discussions, then, reveal even more clearly in recent literature that the considerations involved are really "theoretical" in nature. The literature itself is already asking ultimate questions about the reality of man and giving answers that must often be considered most disturbing in their lack of historical and normative criteria. When we suggest that "theoretical" issues are already being proposed, we mean that such considerations of the results of population increase force the contemporary analyst to fashion a theory of man which attempts to account for the human condition that "must" result in the light of one's views about population statistics. What is of interest here is the drift, so to speak, of these contemporary theories which frankly accept the new man forced into being by supposedly absolute and certain population trends.

Following the presentation of the President's proposals to enable the American Federal Government to enter more actively into birth and population control affairs, the *San Francisco Examiner* wrote a clear and responsible editorial about "the overpopulated earth in peril" (27 July 1969). The editorial pointed out that man's technical mastery enabled him to defy the laws of nature. He could fly, use the elements, control disease. But he had a flaw. He could not "master himself." With little hint as to the enormous history of this very complicated problem of human self-mastery, the editorial found this failure of self-control can lead to a new kind of tragedy. "Unless the population explosion can be controlled, what could be a utopian life in the 21st Century may well become a famine-swept horror." To avert this, what is needed is a program for "birth control devices and information." This program must not impinge "on the religious convictions of any individual," of course, but there seems to be an iron law at work so that without control, "mother Nature may wind up dictating the law."

This editorial — which in its general tenor, could be duplicated in newspapers and magazines all over the world — is a good one for two reasons: first, it is relatively calm and intelligent. It recognizes that the numbers of world population do represent a social and political problem. Secondly, however, there is insufficient fear or suspicion that proposals for population control are not humanly neutral, no matter how much we should like them to be. In short, there really is no large-scale program that does not eventually impinge on the religious and ethical convictions of the individual. If there is anything that is becoming clear in recent writings, it is that population writers find themselves forced precisely to attack religious and humanitarian con- victions as such. These attacks, much more than any abstract fear of nature's reprisals, are the real problems in population theory.

In this context, therefore, two passages which can be taken as representative of many more of the same type can be found in recent writings are here cited to indicate forcefully the more and more commonly accepted consequences of population theory which, since it has of itself no real ethical criterion about the dignity of man, must be based on a theoretical indifference to the question of means.

> One of its (world government's) main tasks, perhaps most important of all, would be the control of population numbers in the various regions of the world. But government requires not merely benevolent good will; it must also be able to enforce its rule by sanctions. What would the government do if it discovered that in some region the population was intentionally being increased beyond the numbers apportioned to it? *It would seem that the ultimate sanction would have to be to kill off the excess.* Is it likely that such an extreme step would ever be undertaken? But if it were not, the con- sequences would be that the world-government would have failed in its main purpose.[2]

In this passage, we find Sir Charles Galton Darwin, obviously caught in the iron logic of his premises, willingly to call into question the historic right to life on no other grounds than it is alive and exceeds the maximum limit. It is brutally clear from

2. Sir Charles Galton Darwin, "Can Man Control His Numbers?" in *The Evolution of Man*, Sol Tax, editor, The University of Chicago Centen- nial Symposium, Chicago, University of Chicago Press, Vol. II, pp. 472- 73. Italics added. (Sir Charles Galton Darwin is not to be confused with his famous ancestor.)

this that the value and meaning of human life is the fundamental issue which lies at the root of this analysis.

The second passage is that of Philip Wylie, not merely because it reveals a trend of thought which receives growing appreciation, but because it is argued in a style that has already transcended the recognized limits of rational discourse.

> The idea that he (man) must take command of his evolution is contemplated by few civilized men. Most meet it with shock, if at all, with resistance, fear, and holy hate. Man belongs to their image of God, they say, and must not tamper with life. (Oh, no?) Adapt the environment to man's present wants, he declaims, and his commercially forced wants, even though supplying them will soon render the environment unlivable. But don't touch life! Life is sacred.
>
> In its human manifestation, life is sacred. Every pushing gobbet of meat extruded from a human womb must be kept alive. Baptized. A hundred able lives must be sacrificed to maintain half as many monsters and all, idiots. A thousand skilled brains must bend their days to find more means to salvage protoplasmic rubbish . . . . Life is sacred according to Christians. Such acts demonstrate the strength and infamy of their beliefs. In their view all men must — and we are — be bound to this sin, even though the gene-pool of men yet to be is daily weakened by the act and seed of such salvaged contaminators.
>
> Life now is sacred because of its immortal soul. The very biology of man that promises what real or relative immortality he may truly have is not even deemed relevant. Let posterity become a deformed rabble but save the souls of blubber-parodies of man, now and forevermore.
>
> Keep the senile living, too, though demented, and at whatever waste of able lives.[3]

3. From *The Magic Animal,* by Philip Wylie, p. 272. Copyright © 1968 by

It may, of course, be argued that these two passages and ones similar to them are exceptions from the somewhat mentally deranged fringe.

However, it is not as simple as that. Quite the contrary, such analyses are becoming more and more accepted in Western and especially American society. In fact, on the premises on which they are argued, they represent the exact logical consequences, however unpleasant, of ideas and movements already firmly set in motion. Recently, many writers in the population field have tried to avoid such dire consequences and still retain the population explosion premise as it is presently being proposed.[4] It

---

Philip Wylie. Reprinted by permission of Doubleday & Co., Inc.

"In late 1967, some thirty nations agreed to the following:

'The Universal Declaration of Rights describes the family as the natural and fundamental unit of society. It follows that any choice and decision with regard to the size of the family must irrevocably rest with the family itself, and cannot be made by anyone else.'

It is painful to have to deny categorically the validity of this right . . . . Some people have proposed massive propaganda campaigns to instill responsibility into the nation's (or the world's) breeders. But what is the meaning of the word responsibility in this context? . . . . The social arrangements that produce responsibility are arrangements that create coercion, of some sort . . . .

Coercion is a dirty word to most liberals now, but it need not forever be so, ... To many, the word coercion implies arbitrary decisions of distant and irresponsible bureaucrats; but this is not a necessary part of its meaning. The only kind of coercion I recommend is mutual coercion, mutually agreed upon by the majority of the people affected." Garrett Hardin, "The Tragedy of the Commons," in *The Environmental Handbook,* Garrett de Bell, editor, New York, Ballantine, 1970, pp. 42-46.

4. Cf. for example, Carlton Ogburn, "Why the Global Income Gap Grows Wider," *Population Bulletin,* 2 June 1970.

"If we wish to make a success of a program of voluntary family planning, time is of the essence. The rate of world population growth is so great — its consequences are so grave — that this may be the last generation that has the opportunity to limit population growth on the basis of free choice. If we do not make voluntary family planning possible in this generation, we will make compulsory planning inevitable in future generations." Richard N. Gardner, "The Quality of Life," *Vital Speeches,* 15 May 1970, p. 469.

cannot be done. In this sense, then, perhaps even more than sufficient analysis of population projections themselves, the great failure to think about the full implications of proposals in population control theory is what may be the ultimate cause of what will turn out to be most against "man himself." The problem at the present juncture is this: what assumptions and developments of thought are required to enable us to arrive at the conclusions of the descendant of Darwin and those of Philip Wylie as though these could be actually conceived as virtue and improvements on the human ethic when, in truth, they are its very denial?

The day following man's first landing on the moon, Werner von Braun remarked significantly, "I think the ability for man to walk and live in other worlds has virtually insured mankind of immortality." [5] What von Braun meant, of course, was that the destiny of man as a race might now be conceived of as independent of the future of the earthly planet.[6] Hannah Arendt had already suggested the philosophical implications of this event in 1959:

5. *San Francisco Chronicle,* 23 July 1969.

6. On a philosophical and theological level, it is interesting to note that Teilhard de Chardin, with more insight perhaps, has recognized that such a projection of von Braun really does not confront the immortality issue:

"If it is a challenge, surely Mankind should accept it. We shall force our barriers, we shall launch our ship on the ocean of space and let the earth sink behind us. We shall, if need be, migrate from planet to planet. From star to star, as they begin to burn out, we shall carry the flame of life. But how will this profit us? Could the last star be less doomed to death than our earth? 'What Titan would prevent Matter from continuing its inexorable contraction and closing in around us? The day will come when the Earth too, like a huge fossil, will sink back into one bleached mass. There will be no more movement on its surface, and in it all our bones will be held.'

'It is not a challenge, then, to a mad duel that comes down to us from the heavens when the nights are clear . . . . It is a final warning.' It is the acceptance of Death, through the trust we put in the Author of Life . . . ." in Henri de Lubac, *The Religion of Teilhard de Chardin,* trans. R. Hague, New York, Desclee, 1967, pp. 50-51.

Should the emancipation and secularization of the modern age, which began with a turning-away, not necessarily from God, but from a God who was the Father of men in heaven, end with an even more fateful repudiation of an Earth who was the Mother of all living creatures under the sky? . . . . It is the same desire to escape from imprisonment to the earth that is manifest in the attempt to create life in the test tube, in the desire to mix "frozen germ plasm from people of demonstrated ability under the microscope to produce superior human beings" and "to alter (their) size, shape and function"; and the wish to escape the human condition, I suspect, also underlies the hope to extend man's life span far beyond the hundred-year limit.

This future man, whom the scientists tell us they will produce in no more than a hundred years, seems to be possessed by a rebellion against human existence as it has been given, a free gift from nowhere (secularly speaking), which he wishes to exchange, as it were, for something he has made himself.[7]

The ultimate issue in population studies is, clearly, over the "creatibility" of man by himself — not so much whether he can do it — he can — but whether he should, would it be really an improvement?

There are, in a way, two levels of action that are proposed in confrontation with this realization. One assumes that the human reproduction of life and of man without the intervention of the "natural" processes of sex and its adjuncts will show that man has not a dependence on anything outside himself. Therefore, to actuate such a change in man would automatically become itself "ethical" because it can be done.[8] No one can possibly grasp

7. Hannah Arendt, *The Human Condition*, The University of Chicago Press, 1958, pp. 2-3. Copyright © The University of Chicago Press, Chicago, Ill., 1958.

8. "We are well aware that this work (fertilization of human cell in a test tube) presents challenge to a number of established social and ethical

the significance of this ever-growing debate who does not understand that this is what is intellectually behind much of the controversy. It is not merely a question of *ad hoc* means or purely practical proposals. Rather, we are dealing with the question of whether
man is a certain kind of being formed, at least mediately, through
the natural evolution of the universe to be precisely man so that
his "condition" is itself the norm of his happiness and his well-
being.

The second level of this argument comes from an opposite,
almost contradictory source. This approach rejects any scientific
reform of man, or even of nature, concentrating on man merely
as just another natural species governed by the same laws as the
rest of the animals and plants. Human laws and codes and technologies based on the uniqueness and superiority of man in nature
are to be rejected in the name of nature itself so that man must
not consider himself any sort of privileged being with respect
to the earth and its resources.[9] This latter is a kind of neo-con-

---

concepts. In our opinion, the emphasis should be on the rewards that
the work promises in fundamental knowledge and in medicine." R. G.
Edwards, and Ruth E. Fowler, "Human Embryos in the Laboratory,"
Scientific American, December 1970, p. 54.

9. Note the way man is conceived in the following passages:
"How much would we give for a rising water table in Texas and Colo-
rado and Arizona, clean, rushing rivers in the great Northeast, a return
of the bluebird to the Eastern Seaboard? How much to bring back to
the Great Plains and mountains our vanishing national emblem, the bald
eagle? to renew the exciting salmon runs and the shad and game fish of
the Atlantic Coast, the deep-water trout and sturgeon in the Great Lakes?
to bring back the joys of water sports and pleasure steamers to the Missis-
sippi and the Hudson? to lift from shame, to regain national pride, in the
storied Potomac? to save San Francisco Bay? to insure our national shrines?
Unless such matters as these become our passion and our priorities, we
shall lose the very meaning of life even as we lose all honest pride as a
people. And unless we find some way to control our pyramiding population,
we shall have to cancel out our dreams forever as we bend to the grim
and slavish task of grinding out new high protein formulas of rock, seaweed,
sawdust, and, yes, crude oil." From *Moment in the Sun,* by Robert Rienow
and Leona Train Rienow, pp. 221-22. Copyright © 1967 by Robert

servatism which uses natural evolution and so-called environmental laws of plants and animals produced by evolution up to now as the norm of the human.[10]

What is common to both of these approaches is their similar lack of a theoretical justification for the being and reality of man himself, for his own central place in the universe, and, finally, for the nature of his intelligence and his hands in relation to his mission of transforming the earth in his own image, indeed, in his mission of improving nature itself. Sir Francis Crick's comment serves as a warning, furthermore, against our confidence

---

Rienow and Leona Train Rienow. Reprinted by permission of the publisher, the Dial Press.

"Scientists of all kinds are warning us most urgently that we are using our technology disastrously, eating up all the natural resources of the earth, creating incredibly beautiful but wholly non-nutritious vegetables by altering the biochemical balances of the soil, spawning unbelievable amounts of detergent froth which will eventually engulf cities, overpopulating ourselves because of the success of medicine, and thus winning our war against nature in such a way as to defeat ourselves completely. All this advice falls on deaf ears, because it falls on the ears of organisms convinced that war against nature is their proper way of life." Alan Watts, "The Individual as Man/World," in *Politics and Environment,* Walt Anderson, editor, Pacific Palisades, California, Goodyear Publishing Company, 1970, p. 354.

The model that governs the Rienows' thinking is obviously 18th and 19th Century rural America taken as a critical norm of comparison, while Watts conceives human technology as hostile to nature, that is, nature is a higher norm than knowledge.

10. "The ecological facts are grim. The survival of all living things — including man — depends on the integrity of the complex web of biological processes which comprise the earth's ecosystem. However, what man is now doing on the earth violates this fundamental requisite of human existence. For modern technologies act on the ecosystem which supports us in ways that threaten its stability; with tragic perversity we have linked much of our productive economy to precisely those features of technology which are ecologically destructive.

These powerful, deeply entrenched relationships have locked us into a self-destructive course . . . ." Barry Commoner, "The Ecological Facts of Life," in *The Ecological Conscience,* R. Disch, editor, Englewood Cliffs, N.J., Spectrum, 1970, p. 2.

that we really know the "nature" which we so eagerly want to make a norm of the human and of environment.

There is also a major problem to which I believe biologists have given insufficient attention. All biologists essentially believe that evolution is driven by natural selection, but someone from the more exact sciences could well point out that it has yet to be established that the rate of evolution can be adequately explained by the processes which are familiar to us. It would not surprise me if nature has evolved rather special and ingenious mechanisms so that evolution can proceed at an extremely rapid rate — recombination is an obvious example. It may even be that if we could look back from 100 years ahead, we would realize that what we know today is not adequate to explain the rate which actually occurs. An exact estimate, if we could make it, using present known mechanisms might for all we know, be out by a factor of 10 or even by one as large as 100.[11]

Thus, not only do we not know the rate of natural evolution, but we also begin to realize that human intelligence as a very intrinsic factor in nature reverses the priority so that man governs nature itself. But human nature itself is not man's to manipulate at will. It is what constitutes the norm of man and nature itself.[12]

11. Sir Francis Crick, "Molecular Biology in the Year 2000," *Nature,* 14 November 1970, p. 614. The British scientific journal *Nature* is probably the best and most scientific source of criticism of the extremes of ecological and population claims and theories, especially American ones.

12. "The most important point in Darwin's teachings was, strangely enough, overlooked. Man has not only evolved, he is evolving. This is a source of hope in the abyss of despair. In a way Darwin has healed the wound inflicted by Copernicus and Galileo. Man is not the center of the universe physically, but he may be the spiritual center. Man and man alone knows that the world evolves and that he evolves with it. By changing what he knows about the world man changes the world that he knows; and by changing the world in which he lives man changes himself. Changes may be deteriorations or improvements; the hope lies in the possibility that changes resulting from knowledge may also be directed by knowledge.

During recent years, Christian theology has been concerned with the question of secularization and with the "post-secularization" problem of hope. The secularization controversy — so suddenly out-of-date already because it was based on a primacy of man which population theory has succeeded in overturning — was based upon the view that Christianity in particular and religion in general were not "worldly" enough. That is, in being devoted to the things of God or of the spirit, man was directly deflected from the true earthly task given to him. This is a type of criticism that is also shared by classical Marxism and serves to date Marxism as well as secularization. Consequently, it was often hinted or proposed positively in these modes of thought that the reason why the earthly task — the construction of the human city — was not yet accomplished was due to the waste of effort by the religionists and idealists in concentrating on non-worldly pursuits. The condition of the secular world — summed up most recently by "the third world" and its development — were raised to the rank of a secular crusade as well as a judgment on Western nationalism and industrialization. "Development," so the current thesis runs, was not transformed into progress, as many had believed would be the case in the 18th and 19th centuries, but into "exploitation" so that the "riches" extant in the world were not due to technology and the spirit that caused it, as the environmentalists say, but to a mere political and social deprivation of other people's goods.[13]

Secularization theology — which is always, even metaphy-

Evolution need no longer be a destiny imposed from without; it may conceivably be controlled by man, in accordance with his wisdom and his values." Theodosius Dobzhansky, *Mankind Evolving: The Evolution of the Human Species*, New Haven, Yale University Press, 1962, pp. 346-47.

13. Cf. the author's "The Problem of Poverty," *World Justice*, December 1963, pp. 198-207.

The best and most forceful argument that the world does not have a population problem but a political distribution problem is Josué de Castro, *The Black Book of Hunger*, Boston, Beacon, 1967.

sically, political — had no alternative in the beginning but to stress and elevate human accomplishments, especially those of technology, to the highest value since they seemed to provide the most radically human solutions and answers to the problems at hand. In this sense, as Hans Urs von Balthasar has remarked, "philosophy has become anthropology." [14] The radical understanding of man gradually conquered the secrets and structure of nature so that nature itself eventually became the projection of man's intellect. In this absolute comprehensiveness of science and its visible successes, we at first found a pressure on religion to come to terms with it. Indeed, it was science that provided the possibility of feeding the vast numbers of the poor and clothing the numerous naked so that a Christian could not even begin to talk about the demands of his faith without becoming aware of his debt to science and techniques.

This stress on science and technology, however, was not totally non-Christian. In fact, there is a very valid sense in which the human dominance of matter and the world is radically Judaeo-Christian.[15] Indeed, it may be more Jewish than Christian in origin, as Leo Strauss has suggested.[16] In this light, what broke down the cyclic, anti-experimental views of Oriental religion and Greek philosophy was the dogma that the earth was created for man and that man was the highest being in the physical world.[17] The connection between science and theology, then, was very in-

14. Hans Urs von Balthasar, *The God Question and Modern Man*, trans. H. Graef, New York, Seabury Press, 1967, p. 27. Cf. J. Metz, *Theology of The World*, New York, Herder & Herder, 1969.

15. Cf. A. C. Crombie, *Medieval and Early Modern Science*, New York, Doubleday, 1959, 2 vols.; E. A. Burtt, *The Metaphysical Origins of Modern Science*, London, Routledge & Kegan Paul, 1949.

16. Cf. Leo Strauss, "Jerusalem and Athens," *Commentary*, June 1967, pp. 45-57.

17. Cf. E. L. Mascall, *Christian Theology and Natural Science*, London, Longmans, Green, 1956; John Archibald Wheeler, "Our Universe: The Known and the Unknown," *The American Scientist*, Spring 1968, pp. 1-20; Karl Heim, *Christian Faith and Natural Science*, trans. N. H. Smith, Harper Torchbooks, 1957.

timate so that there is no way to change the radical pursuit of contemporary science to dominate the physical and psychic world without first destroying its specifically Judaeo-Christian foundations, especially those that claimed — to use the Ignatian formula — that "all things on the face of the earth were created for man."

Up until recently, this belief in the validity of man's mission in the world was taken for granted. The very notion of the development and status of science was based upon the universal acknowledgment of this priority of man over nature, of the proportion between intelligence and the physical world as being intrinsically related to one another as cosmic purpose. Personalism and humanism placed the human being at the pinnacle of human and worldly development and judged success or failure in man's technical and social evolution in this light.

In recent years, however, a very significant change has come into the cultural and intellectual climate of the West. Science is under attack everywhere for a variety of reasons. Population studies, however, are the primary area in which this concept inherent in theology and in modern scientific thought of the dignity of the person and the primacy of man over nature has come to be most basically challenged in contemporary society. Again, it is the tone as well as the content of the panic now sweeping the nation and, in part, the entire developed world over population that reveals to what extent the notion of reversing traditional values has progressed. The columnist Nicholas von Hoffman is again a typical example:

> There is the notion, absurd in the era of the ABM, that having many babies makes us militarily strong. This idea is not only connected with raising cannon fodder for the infantry, but also the masculine definition of virility. You're a man; you really got what it takes, because you can make a female pregnant. *It's going to be hard to convince men that impregnating women is an antisocial act.*
>
> ... Limiting population production will exact other very

large changes. We must divest ourselves of the belief that a
stable or declining population is a sign of a stagnant or de-
generate society. This means a good deal more than accepting
abortion for any reason a woman wants it; it means reorder-
ing our economics.[18]

It remains, of course, for history to judge the truth of the con-
tention that a declining population confronted with other systems
which are growing can remain strong. Certainly the Marxists
seriously question this thesis that the highest sign of progress is
the control of population.[19] Here, merely let us note the remarkable comment that begetting children is now to be viewed precisely as *an antisocial act*. The "natural" has finally become the
"unnatural."

Hence it is, the natural and traditional standards of family
values are coming to be seen as the very difficulties that cause our
troubles. Indeed, it is not too far from the mark to suggest that
population growth is coming to be seen as a form of contemporary
"original sin," the very cause of all evil.[20] The natural love and

18. Nicholas von Hoffman, "Family Size Now the Nation's Business,"
Los Angeles Times, 27 July 1969, p. F2. Italics added.

19. Cf. A. Sauvy, *Malthus et les deux Marx,* Paris, Denoel, 1963.
Cf. also David M. Heer, "Abortion, Contraception and Population Policy
in the Soviet Union," in *Readings on Population,* D. Heer, editor, Englewood Cliffs, Prentice-Hall, 1968, pp. 208-17. Cf. Colin Clark, "World
Power and Population," in *Politics and Environment,* pp. 25-34.

20. "I would say that this vision of the possibilities of fruitful fulfillment
on the one hand as against frustration resembles the Christian view of
salvation as against damnation. And I would indeed say that this new point
of view that we are reaching, the vision of evolutionary humanity is essentially a religious one, and that we can and should devote ourselves with
truly religious devotion to the cause of ensuring greater fulfillment for
the human race in its future destiny. And this involves an all-out attack
on the problem of population; for the control of population is, I am quite
certain, a prerequisite for any radical improvement in the human lot."
Sir Julian Huxley, "The Impending Crisis," in *The Population Crisis
and the Use of World Resources,* Stuart Mudd, editor, Bloomington,
Indiana, Indiana University Press, pp. 10-11.

In this passage, the failure to be redeemed by population control results

devotion of the common man for his children becomes the norm
of crisis and evil. "Whose baby is the population problem?" Rufus
Miles asked. "It is the baby of every understanding, sympathetic
and far-sighted prospective parent who is willing to adopt it." [21]

Consequently, in order to justify those obvious overturnings
of traditional ideas about children, sexuality, and the protection
of human life because it is human life, a new hierarchy of value
must be introduced which returns to the species as a formal concept and which posits the primacy of this species over the person
who is a member of it. Simultaneously with this, there must be
a theoretical manner in which to elevate nature over man's technical capacities, to reverse the notion that nature is for man. In
order to accomplish this, we must attack not only Christianity,
but also science beginning with economics, including the physical
sciences as well since they too have their origins in Christian
theories about the primacy of man over nature.[22]

---

in human damnation so that the besetting, congenital sin of man, as
it were, lies in the area of his control of his numbers. Virtue and vice are
seen in relation to this norm. Huxley, further, recognizes that it is a
religious attitude that is involved, a thought we shall see in another form
presently.

"But the preservation of nature must be defended by other arguments
than reason and our immediate interest. A man worthy of the name does
not have to examine only the utilitarian aspect of things. In our daily
behavior we commit horrible blunders in the name of profit and of what
is considered 'functional.' Nature should not be preserved merely because
it constitutes the best safeguard for humanity but also because it is
beautiful. For millions of years before man existed, a world that was
similar to or different from ours displayed its splendour. The same natural
laws prevailed, distributing mountains and glaciers, steppes and forests
across continents. Man appeared like a worm in a fruit, like a moth in
a ball of yarn, and he has chewed his habitat while secreting theories
to justify his acts." Jean Dorst, *Before Nature Dies,* trans. C. D. Sherman,
Boston, Houghton Mifflin, 1970, p. 328. Here man is described precisely
as the worm in the fruit, which is the parallel in scripture to original sin
itself. Only here it is man who is the sin in nature.

21. Rufus E. Miles, "Whose Baby Is the Population Problem?" *Population Bulletin,* Vol. 26, No. 1, February, 1970, p. 35.

22. Cf. Alfred North Whitehead, *Science and the Modern World,*

The immediate inheritor of the theology of secularization, itself so quickly out of date, was the theology of hope. But hope is known today primarily in its utopian or idealist guise.[23] It has been the function of writers such as Herbert Marcuse, Ernest Bloch, of the Marxist as well as idealist traditions, to serve as a vanguard for the undermining of science and technology pre-

---

Mentor, 1956, pp. 1-19.

In all population discussions, it is interesting how the economist, more perhaps than any other scientist, finds himself at odds with the pessimist attitude intrinsic to so many population studies. The economist is recently more and more singled out for attack from this source. There is a reason for this, of course, which connects the economist to the physical scientist and technologist. For while the latter are rooted in the Christian attitude of the order of the world, the economist is a secular inheritor of the idea of history, especially of progress, and of the notion that nature is for man.

"The life sciences, then, have reached maturity with the amoral pursuit of 'objectivity' that long characterized the physical sciences. Inasmuch as life is intrinsically normative, the contemporary ethical poverty of biology must be due to some more fundamental development that made this distortion seem plausible. I suggest it was the ancient maneuver whereby all nature, life as well as inert matter, was made profane. The maneuver predated modern science by nearly sixteen hundred years. It can be traced back to that point in the Western tradition when both nature and society were secularized. The striking fact is that not science but Christianity turns out to be the culprit.

Prior to the advent of Christianity there had been no secular society and there had been no secular view of nature in Western tradition. On the contrary, as with practically every other known culture, society and nature were regarded as intrinsically sacral. This, of course, was the point at issue between the early Christians and the ancient Romans. The Christian way of stating this was that the one true God forbade their participation in the rituals of any other god. Viewed in the light of today's enlarged perspective, this commandment was preposterous." Harvey Wheeler, "Bringing Science Under Law," in *Politics and Environment,* pp. 312-13.

23. Cf. Herbert Marcuse, *One-Dimensional Man,* Boston, Beacon, 1967; Carl E. Braaten, "Toward a Theology of Hope," *New Theology,* No. 5, Martin E. Marty and D. G. Peerman, editors, New York, Macmillan, 1968, pp. 90-111; Karl Rahner, "The Theology of Hope," *The Theology Digest,* Sesquicentennial Issue, 1968, pp. 78-87; J. Moltmann, *Theology of Hope.*

cisely in the name of the unattained human future. It is specifically the future, *utopia,* that has made the elan of scientific development seem so paltry and even inhuman.[24] The discovery of the "poor" by someone like Michael Harrington or the nobility of the "suppressed" by Franz Fanon and *The Battle of Algiers* have tended to cast doubts on science and technology in the name of man.[25] In this sense, science, which served to displace revelation as the source of wisdom, that is, "worldly wisdom," and revolution, which has replaced "progress" as the cause of the betterment of the human race, and ecological nature, which has replaced man as the norm of morality, all these have combined to undermine the two basic Christian attitudes toward the world — namely, that it is "for" man and that men should serve one another in peace and suffering.

In clarifying the progress of this newer view of man and nature, it is important to recognize that the decline of Christianity, especially in its public dogmatic absolutism, is looked upon as an opportunity for "new gods," gods which prevent or discourage the norms and ideals of the Christian God.[26] The return of "poly-

24. Cf. for example, *The New Student Left,* M. Cohen and D. Hale, editors, Boston, Beacon, 1967.

25. Cf. Michael Harrington, *The Other America,* Penguin, 1962; Michael Harrington, *The Accidental Century,* Penguin, 1965; Franz Fanon, *The Wretched of the Earth,* Penguin, 1969.

26. In this connection too, many writers attempt to analyze the Oriental religions and their spirit as the spiritual answer to the ecological-population problem. Cf. Dorst, pp. 18-19; Alan Watts, *The Book,* New York, Collier, 1966.

"Western man, having adopted the Judaic-Christian religion, has not only banished all living things other than his own species from the partnership of God and himself, but has developed the convenient conviction that God created the rest of living things for the *use* and delectation of man. Orthodox religion may be tottering, but not this mental attitude; so-called rationality even strengthens it. My own plea for a preservation of a natural oakwood drew from a righteous and aggrieved timber merchant the expostulation 'But it's ripe!'

Once life other than human has been relegated to the status of useful

theism," the consequences of the failure of the one God, allows an attitude toward the world and man that is more "open," more in conformity with the post-modern mentality.[27] This prepares us precisely for the return of the non-lubear and non-hierarchic elements in pagan thought. "Polytheism corresponds more realistically to the diversity of our bents and impulses," E. M. Cioran writes,

> allowing them room to flex, to demonstrate so that each is free, following its nature, to stretch forward toward the god that best suits it for the moment. But what undertaking is possible with only one god? What can be made of him? How can he be used? With him around, one lives under constant pressure.[28]

Christianity has lost its firm belief in absolutes, it no longer persecutes, it no longer believes unflinchingly in its exclusive mission.[29]

---

material, or material awaiting the discovery of usefulness to the human being, the return to an ethical system of thought relating to it is very difficult . . . .

Life exists in its own right and this we must acknowledge.

During my lifetime, philosophy, religion and science have come a long way nearer together. The philosophy of wholeness is grasped and accepted, and science now is less sure of any absolute distinction between living and non-living. 'I was born a mineral and arose a plant. . . .' The truth of Zoroastrianism comes back to us, that we are all of one stuff, difference is only in degree, and God can be conceived as being in all and of all, the sublime and divine immanence." F. Fraser Darling, "Man's Responsibility for his Environment," *Biology and Ethics*, Proceedings of a Symposium held at the Royal Geographical Society, London, on 26 and 27 September 1968, London, Academic Press, 1969, pp. 118-19.

27. E. M. Cioran, "The New Gods," *The Hudson Review*, Spring 1968, pp. 439-52. Reprinted by permission from *The Hudson Review*, Vol. XXI, No. 1 (Spring 1968). Copyright © 1968 by the Hudson Review, Inc. For another critical view of this question, cf. Paul Eidelberg, "Intellectual and Moral Anarchy in American Society," *The Review of Politics*, January 1970, pp. 32-50.

28. *Ibid.*, p. 43.

29. Though he reaches exactly the opposite conclusion as Cioran, namely, he concludes that the Christian God might be right after all, Malcolm

In Professor Cioran's view, then, the absolute of this powerful belief in the uniqueness of one's faith is a fatal sign of weakness.

If false gods no longer exist, (as they do not for modern Christians), what better proof have we that our faith is anemic? It is difficult to see how, for a believer, the god to whom he prays and some totally different gods could be equally

---

Muggeridge would agree that there is a great loss of unity and confidence in the institutional church:

"I am well aware, of course, that just to be thus quelled and dominated is far from amounting to being a Christian. In any case, what is a Christian today? One may well ask. From the days when the Very Revd. Hewlett Johnson used to expatiate in Canterbury Cathedral upon the Christian excellence of the late Stalin, to even loftier heights of psychedelic piety, there is scarcely a contemporary absurdity which has not received some degree of clerical, if not episcopal, endorsement. Rebellious or randy fathers come to the microphone to tell us of the doubts which assailed them and of the hazards of priestly celibacy; learned theologians bend their powerful minds to demonstrating that God is dead and his Church, therefore, becomes a useless excrescence. Holy discotheques, sanctified playmates, Bishop Pike of California — dear God! how well I remember him — Bishop (call me, Jim) Pike, and his memorable observation as we made our way arm in arm to the hospitality room from the BBC television studio where we had been doing our little stint of Soper opera. Saint Paul, he said, was wrong about sex. So he was, Bishop, so he was!

One may marvel that, when pretty well every item of Christian belief and of Christian ethics has been thus subjected to some degree of denigration and attack by those ostensibly responsible for upholding and propagating them, congregations of sorts none the less continue to assemble in parish churches on Sunday mornings, and ordinands with seemingly authentic vocations. The Church of Christ has to stagger on under the guidance of those who increasingly are sympathetic with, when they do not actually countenance, every attack on its doctrines, integrity and traditional practices. By one of our time's larger ironies, ecumenicalism is triumphant just when there is nothing to be ecumenical about; the various religious bodies are likely to find it easy to join together only because, believing little, they correspondingly differ about little. I look forward to the day when an Anglican bishop in full canonicals will attend a humanist rally on the South Downs, or a Salvation Army band lead a procession of Young Atheists to lay a wreath on Karl Marx's grave in Highgate Cemetery. It cannot be long delayed, if it has not happened already." Malcolm Muggeridge, *Jesus Rediscovered*, London, Collins-Fontana, 1969, pp. 37-38.

legitimate. Faith is exclusion, a challenging. Because it can no longer detest the other religions, because it understands them, Christianity is through. . . .[30]

This death of the Christian faith, of course, provides the key to a new attitude to man and nature. Nature is released from its intimate dependency on man and can again return to its position of primacy after twenty-four hundred years of subjection to Aristotle and Christianity. The religion that exalted man to his centrality has destroyed him by giving him a burden and a dignity beyond his competency. "And just as paganism had to make way for Christianity, so the latter will have to bow before some new belief; stripped of its aggressiveness, it no longer presents an obstacle to the uprising of new gods; all they have to do is rise up, and perhaps they will." [31] If there is a crucial relation between our attitude toward the protection of innocent human life and our gods, then any radical change in this relationship will see new gods which allow us to take innocent life. One thing is certain, as we shall see further, the dignity and absoluteness of human life are under severe challenges.

The post-Christian, neo-pagan atmosphere of recent times naturally requires a revision in the whole theory upon which the primacy of man was based.

> Obsessed with progress and regression, we implicitly admit that evil changes, either diminishing or increasing. The idea of a world identical with itself, condemned to be what it is, its attitudes fixed for all time, this lovely idea no longer has currency; that's just it, the future, the object of hope or of

30. *Ibid.,* p. 50.
31. *Ibid.* Contemporary discussions of witchcraft, Eastern religions, and new mystical movements in the popular journals of the West would seem to bear this analysis out. This view too should be contrasted with Chesterton's notion of the curious rebirths of Christianity throughout history at precisely times when the intellectuals of an era assume its demise. Cf. *Orthodoxy* and *The Everlasting Man.*

loathing, is our true abode — we live in it, it is everything for us. The obsession with coming events, which is essentially Christian, by reducing time to the concept of the immanent and the possible, makes us unfit to conceive an immobile moment reposing within itself, spared from the scourge of succession . . . .[32]

In Cioran's analysis, we begin to catch the hint of a mood, of a psychology that is, in a sense, both beyond secularization and beyond hope. He rightly sees that both of these concepts, in their secular and religious manifestations, have their origins in the theological past of the Christian West. In this sense, hope, while it may radically relativize the developed present, no matter how advanced it is, is still based upon a goal or a future that can provide a dynamism and a progress which has man, in some sense, as its end point and purpose. Communism itself remains radically Christian in the sense that it refuses to accept the cycles of nature and of man as normative. Indeed, there may be a sense in which Christianity will be protected precisely by communism if these basic values continue to erode in the West.[33]

If we are to detect the theoretical significance of this shift of viewpoint away from theological dogmas that placed man at the center of creation, we must turn, it seems, to the ecologists. For it is from this source that we are beginning to see what is to replace the primacy of man. "In other words, the landscape is not just a supply depot," Professor Odum has written,

32. *Ibid.,* p. 49
33. It is for this reason more than any other that there exists a hope within communism as an historical movement, one that theoretically remains open to the Christian outlook. Cf. the author's "The Modern Church and the Totalitarian State," *Studies,* Summer, 1968, pp. 113-27.

That communist systems do not make a really significant difference in the ecological questions in comparison to other governments, cf. Marshall L. Goldman, "The Convergence of Environmental Disruption," *Science,* 20 October 1970, pp. 34-42; Leo A. Orleans and R. P. Suttmeier, "The Mao Ethic and Environmental Quality," *Science,* 1 December 1970, 1173-76.

but it is also an *oikos* — the home — in which we must live. Until recently man has more or less taken for granted the gas exchange, water, purification, nutrient cycling, and other protective functions of self-maintaining ecosystems, chiefly because neither his numbers nor his environmental manipulations have been great enough to affect regional and global balance. Now, of course, it is painfully evident that such balances are being affected, often detrimentally. The 'one problem, one solution' approach is no longer adequate and must be replaced by some form of ecosystem analysis *that considers man as part of, not apart from the environment.*[34]

What is of special interest in Odum's analysis is not the fact that the being, man, is dependent in some fundamental sense upon the condition of non-human nature — this is Aristotelian [35] — but that man is to be considered as *a part of the environment.*[36] This suggests that the primacy of man is questioned in a new light. He is to be looked upon as a function of something greater than himself in the natural order.[37]

34. Eugene P. Odum, "The Strategy of Ecosystem Development, *Science,* 18 April 1969, p. 266. Cf. also Hugh H. Iltis and others, "Criterion for an Optimal Human Environment," *Science and Public Affairs,* January, 1970, pp. 2-6.

35. Man for Aristotle is the highest of the physical beings.

36. Cf. Charles N. R. McCoy, *The Structure of Political Thought,* New York, McGraw-Hill, 1963, Chapters I and II.

37. Christian philosophy has always accepted that man is intrinsically connected with the world on his material side. This is indeed what man is, the physical being who thinks, but the natural, non-human order was not seen to be the criterion of man, but vice versa.

"At the present time perhaps the most urgent topics for discussion arise out of the fact that science has now made it possible for man to manipulate and transform not only the world of which he is a part but also that part of the world which is himself. The possibility, by microsurgical and other means, of bringing about radical modifications in human genetic material and in the neural material in which man's conscious and unconscious mental life appears to inhere raises novel and complex technical problems for the scientist no less than for the theologian.

As a consequence, in this new approach the quality of the environment — the environment itself or evolved nature — can be looked upon as the prior absolute so that its *de facto* evolution becomes the norm of critical judgment. Anything that disturbs the evolved nature as we historically find it is reprehensible because it interferes with something "greater" than man. Indeed, man is the great predator, he himself, especially his numbers, is the criminal.[38] This means that the classical technological and eschatological mentalities that underpin the primacy of science in the name of the dignity of man are to be challenged in terms of "nature."[39]

This, I must emphasize, is not science fiction; some of these things are happening already. The issues are far from clear, but it may well be that nothing less than the future of the human race is at stake. It may be extremely difficult to draw the line between the changes which would leave the essential nature of man intact and those which would change him into a different species altogether. It may be even more difficult to decide which changes, even among those which leave man's essence intact, are legitimate and desirable. And there will be burning questions as to the people in whose hands the decisions should lie. Both Christians and non-Christians will be faced with problems that they have never been faced with before. But it is clear that only a theology which takes full account of man's radical continuity with the rest of the physical universe on the material side of his being will be able even to enter into the discussion.

Nevertheless, imperative as it is to stress the material element in man's twofold nature, it is no less imperative to stress the spiritual element. If man is not an angel, neither is he a brute beast or a machine. Indeed, it is precisely because man is the being in whom the realm of matter and spirit intersect and interpenetrate that the destiny of the whole material realm is implicated in the destiny of man." From *Theology and the Future,* by E. L. Mascall, Morehouse-Barlow Co., New York, pp. 168-69. Copyright © 1968 by Dr. E. L. Mascall, and used by permission of the publisher.

38. For an extreme example of this attitude, cf. Paul Ehrlich, *The Population Bomb,* New York, Ballantine, 1968, pp. 110-30.

39. This is one of the significant problems with the decline of research and development funds in western society. Man never knows what he can do, but the refusal to progress in knowledge and technology is precisely the ultimate attack both on man and the earth.

Professor Robert Gomer is, then, right to worry about the "tyranny of progress," for progress in the classical sense consisted both in the moral improvement of man through his loyalty to human values and his technological control over nature. Progress in this sense has now become an "evil" since it is precisely these two traditions that have led us to the present population impasse.

> ... We are caught up in an evolutionary stream of our own making but beyond our control. Even under the best of circumstances we will have to accept the fact that man must change to meet changes he himself has set off. Can the process of change be halted? Almost certainly not.... For better or for worse, for a little heart-beat of eternity, until the sun blazes to its death, we who are also part of nature are taking over from nature and are thus becoming our own slaves. Is the tyranny of progress better or worse than the tyranny of nature? I do not know.[40]

A passage such as this, its basic questioning, reveals more perhaps than anything else the degree to which man has lost confidence in himself and his place in the universe. It is ironic indeed that the scientist begins to doubt the very essence of his own background in the name of non-human nature. The combination of population pressure and the commitment to "technology and materialism" are what causes this radical doubt.[41]

Professor Lynn White, in a remarkable essay often reprinted in the past few years, has traced the "intellectual" origin of the ecologic situation. He draws the logical conclusion to this whole recent effort to confront the implications of the population

40. Robert Gomer, "The Tyranny of Progress," *Bulletin of the Atomic Scientists,* February 1968, p. 8.

41. *Ibid.,* p. 4. For quite a different viewpoint of this mentality, cf. Étienne Gilson, "Profets du Mal," *Revue des Deux Mondes,* January 1970, pp. 1-20.

question as it affects man and society. White accepts the Western and Christian origins of modern science.[42] White is convinced that there is a direct relation between theology and environment. "Human ecology is deeply conditioned by beliefs about our nature and destiny — that is, by religion . . . ."[43] Christianity held the distinction between man and nature and further, as we have seen, gave man primacy over nature.[44] The result was that nature lost its sacredness and became a mere tool for man.[45] "By destroying pagan animism, Christianity made it possible to exploit nature in a mood of indifference to the feelings of natural objects."[46] White feels that the ecologic consequences of dogma are visible and chaotic:

> Since both science and technology are blessed words in our contemporary vocabulary, some may be happy at the notions, first, that, viewed historically, modern science is an extrapolation of natural theology and, second, that modern technology is at least partly to be explained as an accidental, voluntarist realization of the Christian dogma of man's transcendence of, and rightful mastery over, nature. But, as we now recognize, somewhat over a century ago science and technology — hitherto quite separate activities — joined to give mankind powers which, to judge by many ecologic effects, are out of control. If so, Christianity bears a huge burden of guilt.[47]

Since it is precisely the application of science that is the cause

42. Lynn White Jr., "The Historical Roots of Our Ecologic Crisis," *Science,* 10 March 1967, p. 1204. (This essay is reprinted in *Politics and Environment* and *The Environmental Handbook* cited above.)

43. *Ibid.,* p. 1205. Cf. also E. B. Fiske, "The Link Between Faith and Ecology," *The New York Times,* 4 January 1970, Sec. 4, p. 5.

44. White, *op. cit.,* p. 1205.

45. This is the essential thesis of the theology of secularization. Cf. Harvey Cox, *The Secular City,* Meridian.

46. White, *op. cit.,* p. 1205.

47. *Ibid.,* p. 1206.

of the problem, supposedly, then further science and technology cannot be the answer in this type of analysis.

As a result, both Christian and post-Christian scientific attitudes are equally dangerous. The conclusions are clear and frank:

> What we do about our ecology depends on our ideal of the man-nature relationship. More science and more technology are not going to get us out of the present ecologic crisis until we find a new religion, or rethink our old one . . . . Hence, we shall continue to have a worsening ecological crisis until we reject the Christian axiom that nature has no reasons for existence save to serve man.[48]

This is the logical and expected conclusion to the evolution of thought we have been tracing behind population theory.[49] It is this new religious or philosophical theory lying at the heart of many

48. *Ibid.*, pp. 1206-07.
49. Professor Lewis W. Moncrief has subjected the White thesis to severe and telling criticism:

"In this article, note is taken of the fact that several prominent theologians and theological groups have accepted this basic premise that Judaeo-Christian doctrine regarding man's relation to the rest of creation is at the root of the West's environmental crisis. I would suggest that the wide acceptance of such a simplistic explanation is at this point based more in fad than in fact . . . .

The forces of democracy, technology, urbanization, increasing individual wealth, and an aggressive attitude toward nature seem to be directly related to the environmental crisis now being confronted in the Western World. The Judaeo-Christian tradition has probably influenced the character of each of these forces. However, to isolate religious tradition as a cultural component and to contend that it is the 'historical root of our ecological crisis' is a bold affirmation for which there is little historical or scientific support." "The Cultural Basis for Our Environmental Crisis," *Science*, 30 October 1970, pp. 509, 511.

Moncrief maintains that other non-Christian societies have had the same problems before the birth of Christianity and outside the Christian orbit. However, the essential problem seems rather to be about the very developmental and evolutionary effect man has on non-human nature itself which is incomplete in itself without man.

population theories that force them always to choose systematically those "facts" which seem to indicate that science cannot solve our problem — often enough quite contrary to the established evidence of science itself — and also to attack the primacy of man in nature.[50] From this we can see that the issue at stake is the ultimate one about the very structure and meaning of man and nature. Population theory is, in this context, the avenue to the return of a more "pagan" mentality, but a paganism without the sense of innocence that perhaps characterized the original.

We are already beginning to see the appearance of this "neopagan" — to find no better word — attitude in population literature, but it is, we must note, a "paganism" of a new and distorted kind. For it is the kind of a paganism that will sacrifice human life to the ideal of the race or the environment. And this sacrifice will be, in its rigorous logic and earnestness, bloody. We have only to recognize the significance of abortion statistics and the proposals of Darwin and Wylie cited earlier to realize that this new moloch is closer at hand than we admit. Another, more profound indication can be seen in discussions of air, land, and water pollution, in the horror with which animal and natural environment are seen to be changed by human necessities and priorities.[51] The dignity of man becomes merely the dignity of those men who are allowed to enjoy the supposedly "natural" environment.

That this new kind of mood is different from the Christian view is obvious. In the traditional Christian and scientific view, *nature was not its own norm but served a necessary though functional relation to man.* Man was the norm of the natural, not vice versa. It was this attitude and the scientific-technological consequences it brought into being that made it possible to refashion the earth in man's name and dignity.

50. Cf. McCoy. The brilliant editorial in *Nature*, "On Which Side Are the Angels," 27 December 1969, pp. 1241-42 should be pointed out here.

51. Cf. F. Fraser Darling, "A Wider Environment for Ecology and Conservation," *Daedalus*, Fall 1967, pp. 1003-19; Barry Commoner, "To Survive on the Earth," in *The Ecological Conscience*, pp. 118-25.

This "neo-pagan" view of the post-technological society reverses this primacy in two ways: first, it elevates the species to the primary position over the individual person and, secondly, it views the species as a function of the "carrying-capacity," as it were, of *nature as it is evolved without the addition of human intelligence as an essential part of evolution itself.*[52] On the theoretical level, an essay such as that of Professor Hudson Hoagland's, "The Unit of Survival Is the Human Race," is indicative, especially in the historical perspective since, according to Aristotle, that which distinguished man from the animals was precisely the fact it was the animal whose "unit of survival" was the race or species, not the individual. When preservation of the "species" was the main object of the group, *individual representatives were to be subject to sacrifice precisely in the name of the group.* The individual as such was to live or die according to the necessities of the species.[53] When we are now told that we must reestablish this species norm, we clearly have come full circle intellectually so that the individual as individual has now no intrinsic reason for existence other than to bear the welfare of the species.[54] On this basis, innocents can morally and legally be sacrificed in the name of the group. Population statistics are then taken to prove that such sacrifice is required, or soon will be.

The intellectual significance of this change can be graphically seen in Professor Richard Means' curious essay, "Why Worry About Nature?"[55] Means too is trying to reestablish a primacy

52. Cf. Garrett de Bell, "A Future That Makes Ecological Sense," in *The Environmental Handbook*, pp. 153-58, where the model of rural America becomes the image of "development."

53. Hudson Hoagland, "The Unit of Survival Is the Human Race," in *The Population Crisis and the Use of World Resources*, pp. 442-49. For an application of this primacy of the species type thinking, cf. William and Paul Paddock, *Famine — 1975*, Boston, Little, Brown and Company, Chapter 9, "Herewith Is a Proposal for the Use of American Food: Tirage."

54. Hoagland, *op. cit.*

55. Richard L. Means, "Why Worry About Nature?" *The Saturday Review*, 2 December 1967, p. 15.

of nature to make man merely a functional part of the on-going evolutionary process which itself is normative over both the person individually and over a particular species as a whole which itself falls into the web of a greater nature. In trying to analyze how man has gained this detrimental superiority over nature, Professor Means' suggests that ". . . the refusal to connect the human spirit to nature may reflect the traditional thought pattern of Western society wherein nature is conceived to be a separate substance — a material — mechanical, and, in a metaphysical sense, irrelevant to man." [56] Now such an analysis is particularly revealing, not merely because it assumes that Cartesianism is "the traditional thought pattern of Western society," but mainly because it misses the whole intellectual point about the classical relation between man and nature.[57]

First, in the Aristotelian tradition especially, both nature and man, because of their regularities, were believed to depend directly upon God or the First Mover for their very being precisely nature and man. Secondly, because man could know and use them, instinctual and non-living nature were directly related to man as his natural supports. Respect for nature was, in this sense, respect for man, because the exigencies of nature physically made man possible. But this respect for nature was a relation to intellect which could understand it, and, therefore, improve it. With the rejection of this relationship — and let us insist again with Professor White, this relationship is the cause of our idea that nature is for man — a new form of what we have called, following the lead of White and Cioran, "paganism," becomes possible. In this new intellectual environment, nature becomes the prior norm, ruling over the human species itself, which species, in turn, claims a higher value than the person.[58] Professor White is much wiser

56. *Ibid.*
57. Cf. the author's "Cartesianism and Political Theory," *The Review of Politics,* April 1962.
58. Cf. Dorst, p. 16.

than many critics when he sees that this is, ultimately, a religious problem which involves rejecting the faith that elevates man to the purpose and center of creation.[59] The issue of man's real dignity and development is, then, squarely joined at this point where faith and reason meet in defining man's true dignity, over the absolute meaning of the human person as such.

A classical contemporary example of this newer priority of nature over man, to illustrate this point more clearly, is found in Robert Ardrey's "The Control of Population." [60] Ardrey's thesis is based frankly on the study of animals. Animal populations do not expand to the limit of the available food supply as Malthus held, yet "no proposition is more demonstrable than the natural control of animal numbers." [61] There is a self-regulatory mechanism seemingly based on possession of territory which determines a

59. The significance of the thought of Teilhard de Chardin is also of great importance in this connection, since it refuses the religious pessimism of the lines of thought we have been tracing:

"We may dismiss, too, the idea that our species may become extinct by dying from lack of food, or through old age, since such contingencies are purely imaginary. Even more untenable is the theory of our 'siderial' migration by astronautics, which people fall back on who have been made to realize the inevitable end of their 'golden age' on earth. These hypotheses either leave the Universe in its present wretched condition, or arbitrarily annihilate it. However, 'we need not rack our brains to find out how the material immensity of the universe can vanish: all that is needed is for spirit to reverse, to move into a different zone, and the form of the World is immediately changed . . . .'

In this we should note, in the first place, how well this view of the 'ultimate end,' unlike gnostic systems and so many other human speculations, conforms to the logic of the Christian faith, according to which 'man's salvation is not an element in the drama of the cosmos'; rather 'is it the Universe, on the contrary, that follows man's destiny.'" de Lubac, pp. 136-37.

60. Robert Ardrey, "The Control of Population," *Life*, 16 March 1970, pp. 24-38.

61. *Ibid.*, p. 24. Again this fails to account for the relation of say the infinite number of chickens that can exist in poultry farms where life and death is not governed by natural predators but by human purpose.

natural, optimal limit for animals.[62] "The great majority of animal species, whether through territorial spacing or sexual inhibition, through infanticide or systematic neglect, succeed in maintaining stable populations year after year." [63] In their search for the causes of this self-limitation, "most investigators today are turning to a social stress as the factor diminishing numbers long before food resources are exhausted." [64] What happens in animal nature is that natural enemies serve to remove the "weak and deficient from the breeding population" so that we cannot remove the natural enemies of any species without hurting the species.[65]

Ardrey then asks if this same principle is not also applicable to man. The principle is, among animals, "that population numbers will never challenge the normal carrying capacity of the physical environment." [66] In pre-history, man regulated his numbers principally by "infanticide or compulsory abortion, by cannibalism, head-hunting, human sacrifice, ritual murder, by taboos against incest or against intercourse during the period of lactation." [67] The newer impulses coming out of the industrial revolution seemingly changed the natural mechanism by which human defectives were weeded out. Humanism destroyed the primitive "mechanism" by which human population regulated itself.

"Humanism's respect for the dignity of man, and its regard for every human life as sacred, while among the most powerful forces ever to advance welfare along certain lines, had ambiguous results on others." [68] These so-called "ambiguous" results lead to such absurd — in Ardrey's mentality — practices as these:

62. *Ibid.*, pp. 26-27.
63. *Ibid.*, p. 28.
64. *Ibid.*, p. 30.
65. *Ibid.*
66. *Ibid.*, p. 35.
67. *Ibid.* Again it is well to note here that Ardrey is again taking a norm from pre-civilized societies as a new goal for modern society.
68. *Ibid.*, p. 36.

"The humanist's preoccupation with the numbers game has sacrificed human quality for human quantity. Life must be prolonged, whatever agony it presents to the dying. A child defective physically or mentally must somehow be saved sufficiently to join the breeding population." [69] So granted that human numbers will never "reach such magnitude as to encounter the limitation of food supply," still the human race on the basis of this new absolutist "natural law" — Ardrey's phrase — has a choice of "a sane and humane program of population control" or "death by stress." [70]

We must inquire what this so-called "humane" alternative might possibly look like in practice, since it rejects explicitly the "humanist" values upon which our civilization was built and by which we distinguished ourselves from the animals who do naturally what we are now supposed to do freely. If we choose to ignore the "natural law" of the animal species and control our population by no plan, then there is a doomsday mechanism which will continue to work to magnify all society's ills — Ardrey, for the record, lists every known current social disease or ill from alcoholism to homosexuality, war and hate — which will overcome us.[71] But men should not be "alone among the animal species

69. *Ibid.*
70. *Ibid.*
"Wars are not fought for personal gain, but out of loyalty and devotion to king, country or cause. The theory that wars are caused by pent-up aggressive drives which can find no other outlet has no foundation either in history or psychology. Nor has the fashionable theory that the phylogenetic origin of warfare is the so-called territorial imperative. Territory means space, and while some wars were fought for actual occupancy of a given space, these were the exceptions rather than the rule. The man who goes to war abandons his territorial home and fights for imperatives which are not territorial but mostly symbolic or abstract: the true religion, the righteous cause." Arthur Koestler, "The Urge to Self-Destruction," *Chemistry in Britain*, 4 April 1970, p. 166.
71. Ardrey, *op. cit.*, p. 38.

to refuse to acknowledge natural law." [72] So they must embrace population control. Just what this entails is of more than passing interest.

Population control, whatever form it takes, is a cultural substitute for biological mechanisms prevalent in the natural world. As our population problem has a cultural cause, so we are provided with a cultural answer. *But the answer must be mandatory.* We have seen that in animal species the numbers of young are not determined by parental choice. A number of proposals for the human species have been seriously put forth by population experts. We must consider enforced contraception, whether through taxation or surplus children, or through more means such as conception licenses, replacing or supplementing the marriage license. Abortion should be freely available to those suffering unintended pregnancy. In international relations, of course, any aid to peoples who through ignorance, prejudice or political hypnosis fail to control their numbers might be forbidden.[73]

Without commenting on the fact that this approach is also fundamentally based on a denial of reason and will in man — again, the lack of reason is the definition of *animals* in Aristotle — Ardrey blithely observes, "such a program sounds more formidable than it would probably prove in practice." [74] We can piously hope that this is not the case for, in theory, this proposal requires nothing less than the totalitarian state.

Here again we see the drastic results in practice of overturning the theory of the primacy of man in nature. Man then becomes just another "animal" regulated by some "natural law" which

72. *Ibid.*
73. *Ibid.*, p. 36.
74. *Ibid.*

he cannot escape. There was a time in the history of thought when the belief that man was merely a grasping animal was popular — Hobbes comes immediately to mind. What we wish to note here is the consequences of the theoretical and practical elimination of the Christian and humanist value systems for the dignity of man and the complete ignoring of man's scientific and technical capacities which he developed precisely to avoid the world Ardrey concludes to be most "humane." What we must acknowledge, furthermore, is that extremists such as Ardrey, Wylie, Hardin, or Darwin are not merely excrescences on an otherwise sane and healthy movement, but rather thinkers who fearlessly carry the conclusions of initial premises to their bitter end. The area of theory remains, curiously enough, the ultimate defense of man.

The drift of population theory, then, is more profound in its presuppositions than we are often willing to recognize. For at bottom, it involves the rejection of the norms and values upon which civilization has been built. And this very rejection is, in the logic of the justifications, required to support the proposals for population control as they are presently being formulated. These proposals, to be sure, are put forth in the name of "man," of human welfare. But if we are rational men, we must be concerned primarily with content rather than intent. We shall see that practically all the necessary notes of human dignity are, in some form or another, denied or distorted in contemporary population theory. There is a kind of diabolic logic at work here which is, in some grizzly sense, both frightening and fascinating.

For we are again confronted with the suspicion that mankind is not ultimately confronted by collective suicide in the form of nuclear self-destruction, but rather he is confronted with the free and deliberate rejection of those forms of life and dignity that make him to be man and not animal, that make him unique and not merely one of a vast number of equally competing species that arose haphazardly in the course of accidental evolution. It seems clear that the intellectual and pragmatic possibility for this rejection of the humanity that God and nature have given to us is now almost complete. Within the context of population theory, as we shall strive to suggest, we are moving, then, to the actualization of this rejection of the centrality of man and his condition in the world.

THE CURIOUS PERSISTENCE OF ABORTION

Perhaps no subject in contemporary society is more controversial and passion-charged than that of abortion. It is right that this should be so since abortion touches human existence and the theories of value that support it at perhaps their most vulnerable and problematic point. What is suggested here is that practically all issues in the population field, by a kind of grim logic, are somehow connected with abortion. Abortion is the great watershed which indicates more than anything else the kind of a thing the human being is considered to be. Abortion is, it seems evident, the avenue by which reproduction will eventually be taken out of the hands of the individual and placed in the hands of the state.

In the beginning, therefore, it is important to understand in a general manner, at least, how this complexity of abortion develops even before treating such issues as food production, scientific progress, or the nature of human sexuality. Here a deliberately strong and absolute position is taken with regard to abortion, not merely because it illuminates more than anything else the issues involved in the whole discussion of human population but also because it is a great evil in itself. For it is around the theories justifying abortion that the shift in the conception of human life and its protection has mainly taken place.[1]

From conception onwards to death at whatever age, the human being is a singular, linear growth. Cut off at any stage, be it at conception plus one hour, plus one day, plus one month, six months, at birth, at birth plus one year or plus fifty years, this particular conceived human life and its subsequent individual earthly history ceases. No other life can be exactly like it. There are then two attitudes that can be taken in regard to the right to interfere with this human development.[2] The one attitude would

1. Cf. Charles E. Rice, *The Vanishing Right to Live*, Garden City, N. Y., Doubleday, 1969, pp. 27-50. Cf. Coleman McCarthy, *"The Worst Kind of Birth Control: Abortion,"* Herald-Tribune, Paris, March 9, 1971, p. 5.

2. Abortion discussions frequently are bogged down by the question, both historical and biological, about when properly "human" life begins so that abortion may or may not be legitimately called "killing a man." In this chapter, I have preferred to use the term "human growth process" or its equivalent, not just to avoid the problem, but to say that I think the problem is irrelevant. Biologically there is not any evidence that this process is not one clear and rapid continuum. The problem of earlier moralists about which so much is made because they felt boys and girls received souls at one or two months after conception seems rather to be mainly an issue of the state of contemporary biological knowledge.

Since there is absolutely no question that the human growth process starts at conception and this growth if allowed to continue results in a human baby, not a cat or a redwood, I take it to be obvious that we are dealing with human life from the beginning. There is a difference between killing a fertilized ovum at conception plus one day, killing the same fetus at conception plus one month, plus six months, killing it at birth, or killing it at forty years of age. It is the same life being terminated. The difference is the difference between killing my grandmother and killing someone I do not know anything about. There are degrees of evil. I simply cannot say

hold that the development of the embyro and the child are con-
ditional things dependent upon the will of the mother, the parents, or society so that the needs of society or the parents determine the right of life to continue.[3] When there is a conflict, the
prior right of the mother or of society comes first.

A second view, however, would maintain that the conceived
human life, at whatever stage, is sacred and inviolable, not to be
destroyed for any reason. In this latter view, keeping in mind the
classical problem of the double effect, no reason of potential
physical deformity, rape, over-population, mental health, or hu-

---

that any life termination is a positive good, though it may be less "evil"
than other sorts of life termination.

Cf. John T. Noonan, "La Chiesa Cattolica e l'Aborto," *L'Aborto nel
Mondo,* Maria Giradet-Sbaffi, ed., Verona, Mondadori, 1970, pp. 117-76.
(Abridgment in *Theology Digest,* Autumn 1968, pp. 251-58.) For a dis-
cussion of the biological facts involved, cf. *The Terrible Choice,* Robert
E. Cooke and others, editors, Bantam Books, 1968, pp. 34-39; Robert
T. Francoeur, "Nuovi Orientamenti nella Riproduzione Umana," *L'Aborto
nel Mondo,* pp. 211-28; Denis Cavanagh, "Reforming the Abortion Laws:
A Doctor Looks at the Case," *America,* 18 April 1970, pp. 406-11; T. L.
Hayes, "Abortion: A Biological View," *The Commonweal,* 17 March 1967;
J. Lavelle, "Is Abortion Good Medicine?" *Linacre Quarterly,* February
1968.

3. "The decision of a woman as to when to bear her children, and
whether to bear them at all, is one which must be the private conscience
of the woman herself, and by the private conscience of a doctor asked
to terminate the pregnancy. Mere moral dogma and especially punitive
repression of sexual union are of insufficient governmental interest to
justify an interference with these rights of conscience.

It is cruel and unusual punishment, forbidden by the Eighth Amendment, to a woman, her spouse and her other children to force her, against
her desire, to bear and rear a cruelly deformed child who will exhaust
the emotional and financial resources of her family." Statement of Howard
H. Jewel, former California Assistant Attorney General and lawyer for
the American Civil Liberties Union in connection with a Hearing before
the California State Board of Medical Examiners, *The San Francisco
Chronicle,* 14 August 1968, p. 5.

John Noonan points out that it was Havelock Ellis (*Studies in the
Psychology of Sin,* 6, 607, 1927) who began to suggest that the fetus was
merely a part of the female body. Noonan, p. 164.

man embarrassment would override the right of the conceived
human process to continue.[4] In the first view, the claim is made
by man over the right of another to life especially when that life
is not yet developed to birth.[5] In the second, society is charged

4. Cf. Brendan F. Brown, "The Crime of Abortion," *Vital Speeches,*
1 July 1970, pp. 549-53; Paul Ramsey, "The Sanctity of Life," *The
Dublin Review,* September 1967; F. Ayd, "Liberal Abortion Laws,"
America, 1 February 1969, pp. 130-32; J. Noonan, "Amendment of the
Abortion Laws," *The Catholic Lawyer,* Spring 1969; J. T. Mangan, "The
Wonder of Myself," *Linacre Quarterly,* August 1970, pp. 166-83.

5. "It seems impossible, or certainly very out of place, to extrapolate
back to the embryo the ethics which we apply to the newborn or the
adult. Conversely, it does not follow that the man who destroys an embryo
will also kill newborn babies. Abortion does not, as has been suggested,
'breach an important principle by suggesting that the deaf, blind and
maimed are disposable.' There is no simple definition of what is human
and what non-human. There is no single event marking the beginning of
life, there is no Rubicon to be crossed during embryological development
upon which we can concentrate and say, 'Before this moment we have
an object as trivial as a nail-pairing; after this time we have an individual
human being to which we must reserve the full sanctity of human life.'
An ethical system founded on biology must begin by recognizing that
reproduction is a continuum which can be traced back to the time when
the primordial germ cells are first recognizable in the yolk sac endoderm
(at about the 20th day after fertilization in man) and it is still incomplete
when a grandmother baby-sits for her daughter's children. During this
long process fertilization is an incident which is biologically important but
so remote from the interests of society that the woman in whose body it
occurs has no way of knowing what has happened." Malcolm Potts, "The
Problem of Abortion," in *Biology and Ethics,* London, Academic Press,
1969, pp. 74-75.

To this kind of analysis, Professor C. B. Goodhart of the Department
of Zoology at Cambridge, England remarked:

"Dr. Potts has argued that human development is a continuous process,
from the primordial germ cell to Granny baby-sitting, and that it is in
principle impossible to define when a new human individual comes into
existence. May I with great respect suggest that this is a view which is
contradicted by biological knowledge? For there *is* a real discontinuity
at fertilization, or to be pedantic at the 'activation' of the ovum which
is not necessarily always the same thing. This is the point after, but not
before, which it becomes capable of completing its development without any
further stimulus from outside. Once activated, the organism will carry

with protecting and caring for all that is human — deformed or not, numerous or not — simply because it is human.[6] The so-called natural instinct of parents to protect their young even at the cost of their own lives is seen to be in conformity with this view of the absolute value of the conceived human as well as the Christian notion that all life is sacred and from God.[7]

Nothing is more intellectually curious, then, than the presence and advocacy of abortion in modern society. Indeed, it is the contradiction in the theories justifying abortion that again causes wonder about their supposed validity. Religion's arguments may not convince, but the abortionist arguments leave little doubt. These contradictions, more than anything else, more than any theoretical abhorrence of abortion, force us to focus upon the values involved.

---

on its development until it dies. That is what most of us would have called the moment of conception, however else the British Council of Churches may now have decided to define the word. But whatever we call it, it occurs at a specific point in time, after, but not before which, development can proceed; and that is a real discontinuity marking the coming into existence of a new biological organism. Whether this point has any special ethical significance may be a matter for debate, but arguments based on the premise that there isn't any biological discontinuity really won't do at all . . . .

May I make a brief rejoinder to Mrs. Mason's point, that a woman has a right to do anything she pleases with her own body? Of course she does, we can all agree with that. But unfortunately more than a mother's own body is involved in procuring an abortion. Whatever anyone may feel to the contrary, it is incontrovertibly a biological fact that an embryo forms no part of its mother's body, right from the start. Whatever else it may be, it is a separate living human organism, inside and wholly dependent, in a sense even parasitic, upon its mother, but no more a part of her own body than a tapeworm would be." "Discussion," *Biology and Ethics*, pp. 101, 103.

6. Cf. E. M. Diamond, "Who Speaks for the Fetus," *Linacre Quarterly*, February 1969, pp. 58-62; Germain Grisez, *Abortion*, Corpus, 1969; Enda McDonagh, "Ethical Problems of Abortion," *Irish Theological Quarterly*, V. 35, 1968, pp. 268-97.

7. Noonan points out that Christian thought about human life stems from the belief that all life is from God and that all life is to be loved by the neighbor as it is. Noonan, p. 119.

We are witnessing a long term separation of sex from reproduction.[8] Abortion, as it is being argued in contemporary thought, is a necessary stage in this separation, the one which eventually accustoms us to the acceptance of the proposition that human life need not always be protected.

In Edmund Fuller's novel, *The Corridor,* there is a passage that suggests the depth of the issue involved:

> I was thinking of that even in the original operation (to remove a dead fetus). There was something awful about that violation and removal . . . even though I knew my child was dead. It confirmed what I would have guessed, but of which I couldn't have measured the intensity in a million years, that abortion must be a hideous trauma for a woman, permanently scarring.[9]

In this passage, abortion is seen as a violation of a basic human relationship — that between a woman and what is begotten in her. What we are now being told more and more is that abortion is an act of virtue with no psychological or moral effects on the woman or society, that the fetus is simply a part of the mother like a finger or a leg.[10] In other words, there is no obligation of any sort on the part of the woman, the parents, or of society to protect what is in fact begotten. The darker side of this pro-

8. "In effetti, dopo secoli in cui l'uomo ha stabilito un nesso essenziale tra sessualità e riproduzione, trovando talvolta la sola giustificazione della prima nella seconda, e ora sul punto di separare completamente questi due aspetti." Francour, p. 224.

"The surprisingly rapid acceptance during the last decade of intra-uterine devices (IUD's) and of steroid oral contraceptives in many developing countries is principally due to the fact that their use separates, for the first time, contraception from copulation, and it is clear that effective birth control methods of the future must exhibit this same property." Carl Djerassi, "Birth Control After 1984," *Science,* 4 September 1970, p. 941.

9. Edmund Fuller, *The Corridor,* New York, Bantam, 1963, p. 164.

10. Cf. Lawrence Lader, "Legalized Abortion: The Final Freedom," *Abortion,* New York, Bobbs-Merrill, 1966, pp. 167-75.

position, of course, is that if society must not protect life in the womb, it may, for reasons of state, take it away, no matter what the mother or parents think.

Abortion is usually discussed popularly in the atmosphere of the "tragic" case — the girl raped by her drunken father, the widowed Mexican lady with ten starving children to feed, the fear of serious deformity, mental imbalance, the Mafia controlled abortion racket.[11] That there is a human tragedy of the highest order involved in abortion instances, there can be no doubt at all. The desire and need to do something about this unfortunate situation is certainly healthy and politically necessary. There is no objection to regulating and controlling abortion in the name of the common good to avoid some greater evil.[12] This is a question of wise means not designed to give moral approval to abortion but to minimize its dire reality. Yet, what is to be done? What happens if abortion is promoted rather as an elementary social right and part of government policy, conceived to be good and virtuous without any scruple? Does the fetus also

11. The statement of the American Lutheran Commission on this question takes this approach for the most part. Statement of Carl F. Reuss, 9-11 1969, in *L'Aborto nel Mondo,* pp. 240-45.

"We believe that no woman should be forced to bear an unwanted child .... the most decisive factors in reaching our conclusions have been our concern that the individual, the family, and society achieve the highest possible quality of life and our conviction that this is unlikely for mentally and physically damaged or unwanted children, for their parents, and for an overpopulated world.

On religious, moral, and humanitarian grounds, therefore, we arrived at the view that it is far better to end an unwanted pregnancy than to encourage the evil resulting from forced pregnancy and childbirth. At the center of our position is a profound respect and reverence for human life, not only that of the potential human being who should never have been conceived, but of the parents, the other children and the community of man." A Report Prepared for the American Friends Service Committee, *Who Shall Live?* New York, Hill and Wang, 1970, pp. 64-65.

12. Cf. R. Drinan, "State of the Abortion Question," *The Commonweal,* 17 April 1970, pp. 108-110.

have a right to continue to live? What happens when we make
this "right" merely a conditioned thing?

At first sight, it might appear that the main point of difference
between abortion theorists and their opponents is over the question
of "wanted" vs. "unwanted" children. Indeed, Lawrence Lader
has argued that widespread abortion would make this "the century
of the wanted child." [13] Anything presumably not "wanted"
should simply be removed before it reaches birth like any unwanted
growth.[14] Such a view is strangely ironic. All life is once fetal,
of course, so that abortion makes continued existence depend
upon sufferance or condition. Thus, the classic view against
abortion also bases itself *precisely* on the proposition that every
child is, in all its growth, to be "wanted." In the Christian theory
of marriage as well as its natural law background, no child is to
be conceived that is not wanted. When this "wantedness" fails
in individual cases on the part of the parents, the whole structure

13. Lader's book (footnote #10) is a too typical example of this ap-
proach. For an opposite view, cf., James J. Diamond, "Humanizing the
Abortion Debate," *America,* 19 July 1969; Russell Shaw, *Abortion on Trial,*
Dayton, Pflaum, 1968; Paul J. Weber, "Perverse Observations on Abortion,"
The Catholic World, November, 1970, 74-77; R. Springer, "Notes on
Moral Theology," *Theological Studies,* September 1970, pp. 492-507; Eu-
gene Quay, "Constitutionality of Abortion Laws," *Linacre Quarterly,*
Spring 1969, pp. 169-75.

14. "Regardless of differences, the movement (Women's Liberation) can
supply a few clear and concrete replies to the question, what do they want
to be liberated from?

The first is abortion law. Repeal of abortion laws has the potential
of such wide support that it is expected to gather otherwise reluctant
converts to woman's liberation.

Of four suits challenging the constitutionality of New York State's
abortion laws that will be heard in federal court here starting April 15,
one case has been dubbed the 'woman's case' because it has 300 plaintiffs
and five women attorneys claiming that abortion laws deny a woman's right
to privacy and her right to decide whether or not to bear children. Control
of her own body is women's liberation's most broadly based tenet." Marylin
Bender, "Women's Liberation: A Fight for Total Equality," *Herald-
Tribune,* Paris, February 10, 1970. Cf. "Abortion and the Law," *Newsweek,*
13 April 1970, pp. 33-39.

of society is designed to make up for the failure in these individual cases so that adoptions, public and private institutions, hospitals for the deformed and defective, clinics for handling illegitimate births, all these are provided to cope with extreme cases in which the efforts of the natural parents are not adequate.

The answer to the "unwanted" child, then, is not its destruction but a new moral and ethical response which creates new ways to counteract individual or genetic failures. All of these institutional, medical, and social responses are direct results of the belief in the sacredness of human life. Without this belief, as we are now beginning to see, such efforts simply will not be made as it is more economical and "practical" to destroy the problem in the first place.[15] Perhaps more than any other area, it is the belief that we should care for what is human that reveals humanity's profundity and compassion.[16]

The curious fact that both the abortion theorists and their opponents agree that ideally all children should be "wanted" children serves to emphasize the structure of thought governing these views. If we should examine the strictest ethical codes, we should find them in agreement with the contemporary abortionist argument in at least this sense: both agree that children of rape or incest, children with serious congenital deformities, too many children, undesired children "should" not exist. Every argument used to justify abortion has its ethical parallel in some more

15. Economists sometimes begin to calculate how much it "saves" to prevent a child in terms of social costs as compared with a life-time of caring for him.

16. Historically, it is of some importance to recall that the governmental origins of movements for the health and welfare of the poor and sick were found in religion, usually Christianity, and gradually secularized. It was the belief that the deformed and the sick must be cared for that led to movements for their care and improvement. Even more anciently, it was the Christian horror of infanticide that led finally to the dropping of this commonly accepted practice. What we now are beginning to witness is a change in the fundamental belief that such a mission to the weak and poor and deformed is worthwhile.

severe moral code designed to prevent the action that caused the unwanted conception in the first place. The force of the abortionist argument is rooted in a despair about human freedom and will. The result of this despair is to place morality in the technical removal of any "untoward" consequences. The anti-abortionist view, on the other hand, places the emphasis upon human freedom and choice as its proper locus. It sees that the fault lies either in the human will or in human intelligence, not in the innocent result of human or genetic failures. One is a consequence, *ex post facto* theory, the other a personalist theory about human relationships.

The Christian theory of sin has an important relation to this discussion. Briefly, this theory would affirm that human affairs are profoundly serious issues because they have consequences which make human life to be, to be well, and to grow. In this light, the conceiving of children outside of a context in which they are actually desired, in which they can be protected, can grow, and be loved was considered to be sinful, doubly sinful indeed because the life of the child was totally dependent on something else besides itself. But, and this is the point, *the sin of not providing this atmosphere resided formally not in the fetus nor in the child,* which could in no sense be considered bad or evil, but in one or both parents or perhaps in familial or societal conditions in which this act took place outside of a context in which it could achieve this desired result.[17]

In the case of purely physical or mental deformities, furthermore, it was considered the task of the parents and society to do whatever could be done for these cases and thereby learn to prevent them. Thus physical and mental deformities too served

17. Canon law itself has its deficiencies here on this point also. The restrictions placed on illegitimate children to hold certain offices were in the nature of unjustified penalties which fell on the child rather than on the parents, even though the intention of the law itself was precisely to prevent illegitimacy.

the social purpose of initiating the medical profession into a search to remove causes of defects. And the suggestion cited earlier of Philip Wylie that efforts to protect and care for hopelessly deformed children and adults are a waste of time must be one of the most degraded suggestions our civilization has heard for a long time.[18]

However, while agreeing with the modern abortionist thesis that children who are not wanted or not capable of being cared for should not, in the abstract, "exist," the Christian theory of sin recognizes that the sole criterion of value is not the intention of the parents or of society. Since what is begotten is in fact, for whatever good or selfish reason on the part of the begettors, in the line of precisely human growth, it is in itself *ipso facto* good and demands protection and help merely because it is human. This is what the right to life basically means and our civilization is surely founded upon it. Indeed, such is our plight, *this is probably the first generation in the history of mankind which is being told that the child itself is the evil and a menace to the human race.* When we consider that the condition of the child has long been assumed to be the touchstone of civility, it is clear how far values have been reversed. This is why the

18. Cf. Philip Wylie, *The Magic Animal,* New York, Pocket Books, p. 272.

It is worth noting, however, that the Supreme Court of the State of New Jersey in a celebrated case in 1967 set down a basic statement about the rights of the fetus:

"If to the child who is about to be born we should ask if we should suppress his life before the time of his gestation is complete in its course, our intuition of human nature tells us that he would certainly almost have chosen life with deformity rather than no life at all . . . . The right to life is inalienable in our society . . . . Thus, while sympathizing with the difficult situation in which the parents find themselves, we believe firmly that the right of the child to life is more basic than their right not to support the consequences of an emotional or financial disgrace." Gleitman v. Cosgrove, cited in Robert B. Byrn, "Il Movimento per l'Aborto negli Stati Uniti," *L'Aborto nel Mondo,* p. 45. Cf. J. Knight, "The Right To Be Born," *The Tablet,* 18 March 1967, pp. 285-86.

belief that the child is the enemy of mankind is, in a sense, the ultimate perversion. Once the human process begins, human society and morality must be designed to respect it and to counter efforts that might jeopardize its growth. The mission of society is to protect and cherish what is human at whatever stage of growth it can be found, including fetal growth and growth that is deformed.

The abortion argument rests upon the assumption first that the species is more important than the individual so that individuals can be sacrificed for the good of the race or society and, secondly, that the fetus is, consequently, good or bad not because of itself but on the basis of the judgment of the woman, the parents, or society about its usefulness or value even after it begins its growth process.[19] In this line of thought, then, the fetus is at least indifferent or even positively evil when its growth runs contrary to any personal or societal values said to be greater than itself. Since this is so, this reasoning allows feticide to be a positive good in the name of human welfare, individual or collective. This means, of course, that conceived human life is only relative. Since there is really no way on this basis to decide — morally or legally — when the fetus is to be protected by the so-called "right to life," the fetus is considered somehow "non-human" until it is viable or, more and more, until it is born. Paul Ehrlich, for example, believes it is mainly "society" not genetics which makes a thing recognizably human so that there is no real reason why it should not be killed before it is born.[20] In any case, we see clearly

19. Cf. above #5.
20. "Biologists must promote understanding of the facts of reproductive biology which relate to matters of abortion and contraception . . . . They must point out the biological absurdity of equating a zygote (the cell created by joining of sperm and egg) or fetus (unborn child) with a human being . . . . People are people because of the interaction of genetic information (stored in a chemical language) with an environment. Clearly the most 'humanizing' element of that environment is the cultural environment, to which the child is not exposed until after birth. When conception is prevented or a fetus destroyed, the *potential* for another human being

enough that abortion is gaining greater acceptance not as an evil which society must tolerate and regulate because it unfortunately happens, but because it is a positive good to be pursued for society's own security.[21]

The difference between a theory of *promotion* of abortion and one of *tolerance* of it is not always easy to grasp. Yet, it is crucial and touches the heart of the issue. The purpose of human government and society is to protect what is human, to provide conditions and norms for its complete growth. The great danger of human society has always been that government can fall into

---

is lost, but that is all. That potential is lost regardless of the reason that contraception does not occur — there is no biological difference if the egg is not fertilized because of timing, or because of mechanical or other interferences." Paul Ehrlich, *The Population Bomb*, New York, Ballantine, 1968, p. 147.

21. The following statement of the American Public Health Association is indicative:

"It is generally accepted that individual women and couples should have the means to decide without compulsion the number and spacing of their children.

This personal right has been supported and enhanced through governmental action at all levels.

The APHA and many other groups have joined with public agencies to secure this right and to make widely available those services that will provide a range of choice of contraceptive methods consistent with personal beliefs and desires.

However, contraceptive methods vary among users in effectiveness and suitability. Pregnancies sometimes occur due to rape, incest, and difficulties in obtaining contraceptives and sometimes because of contraceptive failures.

In order to assure the accepted right to determine freely the number and spacing of their children, safe legal abortion should be available to all women.

Further, the provision of abortion within the usual channels of medical care will reduce the well known adverse health effects of illegal abortion.

To this end, restrictive laws should be repealed so that pregnant women may have abortions performed by qualified practitioners in medicine and osteopathy." *Oakland Tribune*, 14 November 1968, p. 6ES. Cf. also, B. Berelson's thorough essay on the whole field of preventive methods, "National Family Programs," *Studies in Family Planning*, February 1969; "Developments in Fertility Control," World Health Organization Technical Reports, Series 424, 1969.

the hands of men that can kill or regulate human life according to their will. Classical political thought has argued that the only way to protect innocent human life ultimately is to declare it out-of-bounds, so to speak, to affirm that there is something higher than government so that government itself is limited in what it could do to mankind. As we are seeing most graphically today if we read attentively the literature of abortion theory, once we no longer believe in a greater law which protects the human in whatever form it might appear, then the necessary and automatic result is that the right to life is ceded by default to the government or to the individual in function of their own views about needs and requirements.[22]

Consequently, when "the human" seems to go contrary to the temporary political judgment of a given period or nation, since there is no longer anything absolute about protecting "the human" as such, life can be legitimately sacrificed in the name of what appears at the time to be the highest norm — that is, what society thinks it can support according to the cultural norms it assumes valid at the time the decision was made. The pressure on society to grow and expand according to its absolute commitments — which are in the long run the real causes of human progress — is replaced by a "prudential" norm that is bound to its own limited vision. Thus, the killing or not killing — as the Greeks themselves had already seen — is a practical thing to be judged in straight political pragmatism.[23]

Furthermore, on this basis, it is really difficult to see why the Greeks were not more logical in their practice of infanticide, for example, once it is granted that the conceived human life is not itself an ultimate norm. After all, since the reasons for having or not having a child remain the same whether they be used to approve contraception, abortion, or infanticide — once granted

22. Cf. Charles Rice, *The Vanishing Right to Live,* Doubleday, 1969.
23. Both the *Politics* and the *Republic* (and *Laws*) treat infanticide in this way.

that the conceived fetus has no absolute rights — infanticide has the advantage of seeing empirically whether the reasons for not having the child, in the sense of deformity, for example, were valid. If they were, then nothing is lost. If they were not, at least one healthy child could be saved instead of sacrificing two to the doubt.

The real perplexity about contemporary abortion, however, is that it exists at all. Why is it that abortion is more and more proposed as a necessary "right" of the woman and as a positive means for birth control at the very time when science is capable of saving any baby and contraceptive materials should, it seems, eliminate any unwanted conceptions at all? Since logically these two situations should not exist simultaneously, we are forced to find some kind of explanation.

The first and apparently obvious explanation would be that all abortions happen only in those social or national groups in which there is a basic lack of knowledge about or technical means to birth control which would prevent conceptions in the first place and hence eliminate any need of abortions. Yet, this is evidently not what statistics reveal.[24] In all developed countries, in the United States, Europe, Russia, Japan, it is not only or even mainly women who are poor or ignorant who resort to abortion. Indeed, one of the big battle cries is that rich women can easily find abortionists, so let us in equity provide the same for the

24. Stanislas de Lestapis, *La Limitation des Naissance,* Paris, Spes, 1960, pp. 55-106; David Heer, "Abortion, Contraception and Population Policy in the Soviet Union," *Reading on Population,* Prentice-Hall, pp. 208-17; Irene B. Taeuber, "The Population of Japan," *Population: The Vital Revolution,* Doubleday Anchor, 1964, pp. 215-26.

Abortion statistics are never wholly accurate, but it seems that a figure of about one million per year would be reasonably accurate for the number of abortions in the United States and Western Europe per year. Japan has ranged from one to two million per year for over twenty years. Russia seems to have a very high abortion rate as do the Eastern European countries. However, Frank Ayd has justly pointed out the propaganda use these figures can be subject to. Cf. *America,* 1 February 1969.

poor. In the United States, the women who have abortions must
be assumed to be mainly intelligent and possessing some economic
standing. "Every state in the U. S. has a law governing abortion,
most of them prohibiting it under all but the most extreme circumstances. Yet, last year more than a million American women
had abortions — all except a few thousand of them illegal . . . .
Contrary to popular notions, most women who seek abortions
are married. More than half are over 21." [25] So it must follow
that conceptions (obviously the necessary preludes to abortions)
are not merely the result of lack of knowledge or unavailability
of means of contraception. The essential problem is rather why
contraceptives were not used in fact when they were available,
and why is it that abortion is coming to be considered as simply
another form of contraception to be used as a final check when
chemical or mechanical means fail?

This same evolution is evident in another way. Organizations
and movements which have long been concerned with so-called
"family-planning" are now rapidly turning to abortion as an
essential aspect of their programs. Indeed, there seems to have
been in recent years a kind of despair set in among these groups
which find the hope once placed in the success of contraceptives
more and more groundless and this not on religious grounds
or moral attitudes but simply on the basis of the evident fact
that people will not use contraceptives with enough certainty.[26]
The recent turmoil over the safety of the pill has only turned
attention to abortion more forcefully.[27] However vast and simple
the array of contraceptive "means," there is a growing panic
about their real effectiveness so that abortion is now looked

25. "Abortion Comes Out of the Shadows," *Life*, 16 March 1970, p. 10.
26. The Planned Parenthood Association itself seems to be growing
aware of this and has now begun to opt for the promotion of abortion on
demand as a normal part of its program. Cf. also, "Abortion Counselors:
Clerics Help Women End Unwanted Pregnancies," *The Wall Street Journal*,
June 23, 1969.
27. Cf. #25.

upon as an absolute requirement.[28] Propagandists such as Paul Ehrlich and the Paddocks are much more frank and open about this topic, freely admitting that family planning cannot be successful so that the more drastic consequences must be accepted. This seems to be also the growing testimony of the people most intimately involved in the population and welfare problems of public life.

The point is not that contraceptives — which until recently have been, somewhat illogically perhaps in view of the implied norm of this preference, considered to be more effective and "humane" means of birth and population control — do not or cannot prevent conceptions in particular acts. They can and do. But the failure rate of contraceptives is not mainly due to a mere "technical" failure or faulty equipment. It is quite clearly recognized that it is a failure of the agents involved so that the problem lies in the area of the control of the persons who are supposed to be using the preventative means. Because there is such a growing doubt about the efficacy of the human agents as human, that is, as exercising will and intelligence, coercion is becoming more of an open issue in family size and population discussions.[29]

28. For a survey of the various contraceptives being proposed and the public policy on family planning in general, cf. "United States: Report on the President's Committee on Population and Family Planning," *Studies in Family Planning*, April 1969; Sheldon J. Segal, "Contraceptive Technology: Current and Prospective Methods," *Reports on Population/Family Planning*, October 1969.

29. Cf. Ehrlich, p. 81; William and Paul Paddock, *Famine, 1975!* Boston, Little, Brown and Company, 1967, p. 23ff.

"And population control, of course, is the *only* solution to problems of population control," Ehrlich, p. 146. Ehrlich's book is in fact a basic primer on the totalitarian implications of his own proposals.

A more sophisticated but no less clear statement is that of Alice S. Rossi: "But an even more difficult problem must be faced. Demographers have investigated how many children young couples want to have, and how large a family they consider 'ideal.' The results pinpoint the major dilemma facing the rapidly expanding human population: people want too many children. Permitting women to abort unwanted pregnancies is one very small step toward reducing population growth rates. The much

Conceptions occur not merely because the technical apparatus or pill or IUD had failed — this can happen too, of course, though the failure rate is statistically rather small — but largely because the contraceptives were not used. And this is a voluntary problem. Here, it seems, we touch something much deeper in the human, something that makes it appear in a way that even abortion is a lesser evil than the trouble it takes to prevent conception. In other words, the sexual act that is given by nature within which openness to conception is at least a possibility is, in practice, preferred to be left unhindered in a sufficient number of cases to cause a high incidence of conceptions even in those who have no moral problem with contraceptives themselves or no economic or intelligence problem about their cost or use.

The willingness to leave the conceptive act unhindered even at the cost of a potential abortion seems to give the act more personal meaning, perhaps as a sign of love or trust, even though the shadow of abortion in the long run violates this belief.

Furthermore, when abortion is considered normal or acceptable, it is not so necessary to take the required means to prevent conception so that less care will be taken with contraceptive means since there is always the ultimate backstop of abortion made ever easier and cheaper in modern society. If we consider in detail the arguments and reasons given for the necessity to use and employ contraceptives, these same reasons remain essentially the same and valid even when contraceptives fail to achieve their

---

more difficult but more effective solution must be a reduction in the rate of wanted pregnancies." "Abortion and Social Change," *Dissent*, July-August 1969, p. 341.

There is no question that in recent years this whole discussion has quickly shifted from the problem of plurality and tolerance of diverse "opinions" to the problem of coercion of erroneous consciences (that is, those beknighted souls who want children) in the name of a so-called higher good.

Cf. the articles of Djerassi, no. 8 above and those of Carlton Ogburn and Rufus Miles in *Population Bulletin*, 2 June 1970 which seek to avoid this consequence.

purpose, whatever the reason for the failure, unless there is something about the fertilized ovum in its growth that is absolute and sacred apart from the will of the female or male involved in the conceptual act or apart from the desire of society in general.[30]

If this belief in the human context of the conceived human process is not accepted, there is every reason to destroy it at some stage in the growth since the so-called reasons for not having the child remain in that case valid in themselves.

The ethical concept of the difference between the reasons for not wanting a begotten fetus to grow to maturity based on parental or societal reasons and those based on the sacredness of what is begotten, no matter what the subjective intentions of the parents or society, is, therefore, fundamental. It may well be, as we have suggested, that the advocates of abortion and its opponents might agree that a particular conception should not have taken place. But when a conception has happened for whatever deranged or felicitous or accidental human reason or for whatever failure in the biological processes, the right of the fetus, the process of human growth, becomes paramount. That is why, ultimately, modern abortion requires a new religion for it must hold — contrary to scientific evidence — that the fetus has no element of the human that demands absolute respect or at least not enough actually to protect it.

To kill such an incipient human fetus (the word usually used is "interrupt," as it seems more ethically neutral) does require another religious attitude, and this is why the passion and even coercion, of which Professor Cioran spoke, is now found displayed over this question, both by advocates and opponents of abortion.[31] From an historical point of view, furthermore, what is especially

30. Cf. Noonan, pp. 175-76. The statements of the United States Bishops, 21 April 1969 and the Canadian Bishops, August 1968 are based on the same approach. *L'Aborto nel Mondo,* pp. 229-39.

31. Cf. E. M. Cioran, "The New Gods," *The Hudson Review,* Spring 1968, pp. 39-40.

noteworthy is that this new religion is, in many respects, very much like the ancient heresies of Manicheanism or Albigensianism which held the living matter of man to be itself evil and therefore capable of being hated or destroyed.[32] This very hatred of the body and of matter was, like modern abortion, considered to be an act of virtue.

It is widely held, especially in religious circles unaware of the rapid change in the ethical climate of recent years, that there is simply no connection between contraception and abortion.[33] Even to suggest that there might be a connection meets with absolute refusal to consider the possibility. Since the unrelatedness is believed to be the case, the problems of abortion and contraception are considered to be separable and unrelated issues. However, it remains unexplainably true that if the arguments of the contraceptive theorists — as opposed to frank abortionists — were obviously valid, there simply should be no abortion among those classes of people with intelligence and financial capacity to acquire and use these preventive means. But the facts seem to suggest that these very classes still require abortion and on an ever increasing scale in spite of improvements in contraceptive technology.

It seems to be an intellectually fascinating fact, then, that no matter how liberal abortion laws are made, the illegal and illegitimate abortion rates remain appallingly high. Country after country which have easy abortion laws experience this phenomenon.[34]

---

32. Cf. Denziger, #241-42; 428-30.

33. I do not wish to suggest, of course, that necessarily anyone who fails in contraceptive efforts automatically resorts to abortion. Many do, many do not. Indeed, the absolute will not to resort to abortion changes, it seems to me, the most objectionable aspect of contraception from a practical point of view. It is still important, however, to be for or against abortion for a clear intellectual reason; what ultimately matters is the intellectual reason why it is or is not legitimate.

34. de Lestapis, p. 60ff. Again this does not mean that some contraception is not successful in its immediate aim, but it means rather that the failure rate is high enough when there are no further values involved

The movement for "abortion on demand" is merely the logical consequence of this situation. This is why population experts are turning to sterilization and widespread abortion. It seems that the argument about the desirability of contraception over abortion is not being accepted on a sufficiently large scale so that we must, in some basic sense, question the validity of the belief that no connection exists between abortion and contraception.[35]

The belief that contraception is more ethically good than abortion rests upon some kind of an implied belief in the value of the begotten human process. If this human growth sequence does not begin, obviously no human "life" can be destroyed. If, however, there is no ethical absolute about the human conception, then contraception and abortion are equally valid and differ only in the question of taste or preference. The weakness of the theory that contraception has nothing to do with abortion lies not only in the statistics about abortion among groups which should logically be preventing conception rather than having abortions, but in the question of intention. Contraception requires also an *intention* sufficient to overcome a distaste to interfere in some manner with the natural sexual act which in practice is

---

to insure a perennial number of pregnancies which are terminated no matter how liberal the abortion laws. Abortion on demand theoretically eliminates this problem, but it immediately introduces other questions of population stability, age, and security. Cf. the discussion of the Anglican Bishops, *L'Aborto nel Mondo,* pp. 17-35.

35. In the abstract, there is no question, it seems to me, that contraception is more "ethical" even by traditional standards than abortion. It would really be a healthy sign if abortions were eliminated by contraception. The fact that they are not is, to repeat, one of the most paradoxical aspects of this whole debate, so unexpected and illogical that it cannot be totally ignored as an intellectual problem. Cf. the author's "Christian Political Approaches to Population Problems," *World Justice,* #3, 1966-67, pp. 301-23. Cf. also, Winfield Best and Louis Dupre, "Birth Control," *Encyclopedia Britannica;* L. J. Suenens, *Love and Control,* Westminster, Md., Newman Press, 1960. The journal *Child* & *Family* is also a continuing source of material on this topic as is the French Journal *L'Anneau d'Or.*

always preferred to an act encumbered in some sense with contraceptives, including the pill. This intention, and the acts following from it, is designed to prevent conception in the particular act (where conception takes place) so that what is accidentally conceived, contrary to the intention, is specifically *not* wanted. It is this "intention" not to have a child, as it were, that jeopardizes the fetal life, since actual conception does not of itself change the reason for its avoidance in the first place.[36]

It is, to be sure, possible to argue that contraception is rather like rhythm in which the intention must also be considered. But in the case of rhythm there is a difference, for its ambiente proceeds on the assumption that, while a pregnancy is not wanted at the present time, still if it happens, the basic "intention" of the relationship falls within the context of those things that are wanted. That is what the structure of the act is about. Thus the intention is to protect and want what is conceived in fact even if conception may not have been wanted particularly at this or that given time. Contraception and rhythm would, in this sense, only differ in a minor point of efficiency if the absolute will to protect what is begotten is present and if there were no relation between the contraceptive intention and the willingness to sacrifice

36. Gabriel Marcel has touched the essential issue:
"Let us take, for example, the case of contraceptive means. . . . To the believer, it is of first importance, if not exclusive importance that the man and the woman, as begettors, limit themselves to assuring the conditions in which there is incarnated a human being who is as such an image of God. That which counts above all is the gift emanating from God to whose service human beings ought to open themselves. It seems to me that only by recognizing this gift is it possible to grant to life, or, more exactly to the transmission of life, a sacred character. But the manipulation of life which every anticonceptional activity imports seems to imply an abstraction from this gift, that man considers himself no longer a mediator but a producer. We hold further that this mediation is bound to creation; so each human act should be rather considered mediating than creating." Gabriel Marcel, "Il Sacro nell'Età della Tecnica," *Il Mondo di Domani*, P. Prini, editore, Roma, Abete, 1964, pp. 86-87.

life when the prevention fails.[37] However, the fact that the contraceptive act is structured to avoid pregnancy makes it partake of itself not so much of rhythm but rather of those acts which are intrinsically infertile, that is, those acts which absolutely separate sex from reproduction even in the natural order.

Now it is important to consider in some sense those sexual acts which positively separate reproduction and sex — the separation that more and more clearly represents the movement of modern times. The acts which perform this separation most thoroughly and efficiently are, of course, homosexual or lesbian acts in which there is "sexuality" with no natural possibility of reproduction. There is no "seriousness" in such acts because they cannot have an effect upon the material world. They are, in a sense, "in vain." And if such acts are intrinsically "in vain," then sexuality of theoretical necessity, as Gore Vidal has often and correctly implied, must be expanded to include within its area of legitimacy and normalcy all sexual acts of whatever sort.

Until this generation, tribal moralists could argue with perfect conviction that there was only one correct sexual equation: man plus woman equals baby; anything else is wrong. But now that half the world lives with famine and all the world by the year 2000 if Pope Paul's as yet unborn guests are allowed to attend the "banquet of life," the old equation has been changed to read: man plus woman plus baby equals famine. If the human race is to survive, population will have to be reduced drastically, if not by atomic war, by law, an

37. However, this does not take into consideration the psychological aspects of the act and the relationship which may find precisely this difference to be founded in the natural structure of the act. This seems to be one of the major reasons why contraceptives are in fact not used so that so-called unwanted pregnancies result from the more powerful attraction of the natural act left operative without contraceptives. Cf. Max Levin, "Sexual Fulfillment in the Couple Practicing Rhythm," *Child and Family,* Winter 1969, pp. 5-13.

unhappy prospect for civil liberties but better than starving to death. In any case, it is no longer possible to maintain that those sexual acts which do not create (or simulate the creation of) a child are unnatural . . . .

Nevertheless, despite contexts, we are bi-sexual. Opportunity and habit incline us toward this or that sexual object. Since additional children are no longer needed, it is impossible to say that some acts are "right" and others "wrong." [38]

Vidal sees clearly that if sex and reproduction are separable, then there can no longer be a hierarchy in sexual matters. If the two do not somehow belong together, then there is no sense in objecting to any kind of "sexual" activity.

The significance of this thesis should not be passed over lightly. For it is a logical and consistent result, as we shall see more fully in the next chapter, of removing the distinction in things. If man is a certain kind of a being, created in a definite manner such that his heterosexual structure (which, contrary to Vidal, is itself now problematic as the geneticists rightly suggest) is part of the definition of what he is, then the denial of his uniqueness in nature and history can only result, as it is resulting, *in the identification of sexuality with all things that are sexually possible.* There can no longer be a distinction between virtue and vice, in terms of sexuality itself. If mankind is not a definite, formed being, then his full participation in his own reality would have to include his *doing* all things available to him. In the sexual field, this would mean to do all those things in any sense considered "sexual." Otherwise, he could not be considered a full human being.

The difference between this and classical thought lies in the fact that there was a distinction between virtue and vice, based precisely on the relation to normal sexuality and reproduction.

38. Gore Vidal, "On Pornography," *A Thirsty Evil,* New York, Four Square Books, 1956, pp. 121-23.

Virtue meant following these lines of nature; vice meant deviating from them. And the deviation was seen as the destruction of "the human." In the current theory, there can be no specifically "wrong" sexual thing, except perhaps the being cut off from the whole variety of sexual experience other than the traditional "normal." The paradox is the traditional "normal" did just this. It cut man off from all sexual experience except that related to the woman within the overall context of children. The most "sexual" being thus was the one who avoided all the deviations because they jeopardized the optimal sexual experience found alone in matrimony.

When sex is not to be considered intrinsically related to children in some broad sense, its purpose and being are then the results of merely their own experience. They are inert with regard to the potential life-giving capacities of the race. Abortion is only the ultimate and logical conclusion of the theory that sexual acts should essentially be separate from reproduction for conception contrary to positive intention is, in this view, truly "unnatural" and should be eliminated since what is conceived has no intrinsic right in itself. Indeed, while abortion merely completes the "intention" not to have a child, it is necessary in a society like our own because people still insist on using those sexual acts that *might* produce children. The totalitarians among us are beginning to get the message. Thus, too, in a sense, the homosexual theorists have a point. It does seem to make reasonable the view that sexuality without the possibility of children is more ethical than sexuality which takes the chance of resulting in conception when it is precisely conception that is to be avoided.

The theoretical and actual statistics of abortion in a society are a remarkably good indicator of that society's view of human life. For abortion represents the end product of failures in contraception (or failures of responsibility for what is begotten). Those who believe that the human fetus should be protected are not the ones who resort to abortion. So abortions are contraceptions of whatever variety that failed either because the means did not work or because the couple preferred not to use the known means. (Thus rhythm is also 'contraceptive' when the persons involved intend to resort to abortion should rhythm not work in a particular case.)

In either case, then, actual abortion suggests that responsibility for the act of conception was not part of the intrinsic structure of the act. Indeed, conception is more of the nature of a violation, an infringement so that the bond between the man and the woman comes to be represented by the very destruction of what has resulted in their personal relationship. Love in such a mentality becomes visible not in the child, but in the process of its destruction which is believed to be in the best interests of both. And this becomes the ultimate norm. This is the ultimate reduction, the overturning of the meaning of human love which was designed precisely to protect human life by assuring the couple that what happened between them was significant and creative beyond themselves.[39]

When human life is no longer precious enough to be the sign of a mutual relationship and value to be protected against the world itself if need be, the stage is then set for a transference of the reproductive capacity to society itself and a restriction of sex to purely private purposes. Plato, in a sense, accomplished this same end by a theory of state control and selective breeding. We have now the beginnings of a much more modern and more sinister version of this same approach. As we shall see in the

---

39. The lengthy discussions in current moral theology about the primary and secondary ends of marriage, or rather their fusion into one norm are valid enough. Obviously not all sexual acts end in reproduction and this does not render them meaningless. What the fundamental issue is, however, remains the same in a sense, namely, what is the precise difference between naturally unreproductive acts such as those connected with homosexuality and those which are in fact unproductive but not homosexual? The overall climate and context of relatedness to children seems to me to be the primary biological and moral factor.

following chapters, it is both amusing and tragic that the result of sexuality in the modern world is ending in its very elimination, in the transferral of its results to science and the state.

We should not, then, mistake the significance of the modern facts and theories about abortion. Its widespread justification and practice must eventually mean the removal of the generation of human beings from the traditional family, from the husband-wife structure of man. For when the destruction of the human life process becomes itself a positive good, then there is no reason why the unit designed primarily for the protection of human life through human love should continue when it is precisely this life and love that are supposed to be modern threats to man. We are already beginning to have some of this in corporate family theories.[40] Vidal was undoubtedly right. If, in modern times, man plus woman equals baby equals famine or any other undesirable result, then it makes sense to get rid of the initial equation — which the geneticists as well as Vidal tell us is both possible and logical.

40. Cf. George B. Leonard, "Why We Need a New Sexuality," *Look*, 13 January 1970, p. 54; B. F. Skinner, *Walden II*, New York, Macmillan, 1966.

INTELLECT, ANTI-INTELLECT, AND THE SEXUAL REVOLUTION

Sex and intellect are both topics sufficiently interesting in themselves to deserve considerable attention, an attention neither evidently lacks in the modern world. Furthermore, the presumption to treat them together may very well sound pretentious. In a sense, nothing worse can be imagined than a highly abstract discussion of sex, unless perhaps it is the naive reduction of theological or philosophical categories to sexual terminology. Yet, there are trends and elements in the modern sexual revolution that do pretend to serious intellectual aspirations. And these movements merit some consideration as they occupy a crucial point in the theory of population and human dignity.

Ethical philosophy has always been fully aware of the close connection between the human passions and the intellect. When he spoke of sensuality, Thomas Aquinas, along with Aristotle, displayed a rigorous intellectualism. The intellect was the superior power in man, his defining characteristic. Thus, any tendency contrary to reason was a serious sin, that is, a serious violation of human dignity, but only if it was so judged by the intellect.

> The consummation of sin, however, is in the consent of the reason — we speak here of human sin, which consists in the human act whose principle is reason. Whence, if there is a beginning of sin only in sensuality and it does not proceed up to the consent of reason, the sin is not serious because of the imperfection of the act.[1]

The example Thomas gives of this relation between reason and passion is the standard one of adultery. "So in the case of adultery, the concupiscence which consists only in sensuality is not a serious sin, if however it follows through to the agreement of the reason, it is a serious sin." [2] In this consideration, the superiority of the intellect over the senses does not deny the legitimate tendencies of the senses themselves. Even adultery, then, if it is not a freely and fully understood decision, is not a serious violation of human relationships because the senses are naturally attracted to their objects, and it is not wrong for them to perform their normal functions. The purpose of the intelligence is not to take the place of or destroy the senses, but to guide them to their own proper purposes in conformity with the general goals and needs of the whole person.

The significance of this relationship between reason and the senses cannot be overestimated, for it is the foundation of all theoretic discussion about the significance of sex in the modern world. The issue is, in a few words, a metaphysical one in so far as the varied elements that go into making sexual freedom and reformation are considered to be more than mere degeneracy but rather a statement or belief in the nature of reality

1. II-II, 35, 3.
2. *Ibid.*

itself. For there exists in the mind of many theorists a very close relation between sexual revolution and political, even metaphysical revolution. Herbert Marcuse, for example, in an interview about student unrest in Europe and America, has suggested what he believes to be involved in these movements:

> It is a rebellion at the same time moral, political, and sexual. A total rebellion. It finds its origin in the depths of the individual. These young people no longer believe in the value of a system which seeks to uniformize and to absorb all. In order to live an existence governed by instincts which have been finally liberated, the youths are disposed to sacrifice many material benefits. These young rebels already personify a new type of man, a new Adam.[3]

Marcuse's analysis is significant because it deliberately associates moral, political, and sexual rebellion as aspects of the same phenomenon. All of this has the purpose of forming a supposedly "new man," *a new Adam,* the man with no history, the man who has wiped his hands of the morals and values of the past which are said to be the causes of the world's ills. The making of man anew, the overcoming of what he is as received from nature then is to become the project for humanity so that there will be nothing left of his "sinful" past.[4]

Since it is in fact "history," the physical link of the generations that makes us as human beings all one and enables man to participate in the actual world that does exist, the new Adam must be conceived as a rejection of the link of history.[5] Even

3. "Intervista con Herbert Marcuse e Mauro Calamandrei," *L'Espresso,* 24 March 1968, p. 6.

4. There are perhaps two ways to conceive this. In the first, it is science and technology that become the cause for the removal of the human which causes evil. In the second, non-human nature is taken as the norm of the good so that evil arises from its human disruption.

5. In this sense, both technology and nature minus man reject history as a factor in human dignity.

more, there is a deliberate turning away from the intellectual norms
which are said to form man into the kind of a being he is, the
norms of reason and the institutions of family and state that
have the task of supporting the historical human structure. For
this reason, it is precisely by overturning the so-called ethical
norms of sex and authority that human autonomy is achieved.
With these defining norms that keep traditional man to be man
gone, man can be said to establish himself as a new being, a
new Adam, whose new generation will not pass on original
sin and its inheritance which is seen to have been associated with
those who belonged to the race of the old Adam, a race incurably
infected with wars, hatreds, passions, population growth, and
weakness.[6] But the terms of the modern sexual, political, ecological, and intellectual revolutions have their dark sides to them
because their results always seem to be attacking the very possibility of man as we have known him. There is a sense in which
the defense of what man is, then, does depend on the receiving
of him as something created to be precisely man from nature.

The revolution of sexual and ethical thought provides some
striking indications of the importance of man's basic being. The
levels of this "erotic revolution," as Lawrence Lipton has called
it, are indeed varied. "Again, as in all revolutions," he writes,
"the erotic revolution has reached the point today where it is no
longer the parent or even the law — which is being ignored, defied
or flouted on every hand by the sexually liberated — but the
individual himself who is the last barrier against cultural change." [7]
Thus, there are philosophical, theological, and social overtones
connected with this issue. The literary form of this revolution is
primarily poetry, the novel, the theater, the film. Allen Ginsberg's
now famous poem, "Howl," stands, in a way, both as a prophecy

6. Cf. the author's discussion of this point in "Caesar As God," *The
Commonweal*, 6 February 1970, pp. 505-10; "Spirituality and Politics,"
Worldview, July/August 1970, pp. 12-16.
7. Lawrence Lipton, *The Erotic Revolution*, Los Angeles, Sherbourne
Press, 1965, p. 112.

and a sign of this movement as it includes both homosexuality and rebellion as signs of the new man's rejection of the historic past.[8]

> I saw the best minds of my generation destroyed
>> by madness, starving, hysterical, naked . . .
> dragging themselves through the negro streets at dawn
>> looking for an angry fix . . . .[9]

The "madness" has as its major cause the society inhibited by the supposed restrictions of classical morality.[10]

In recent years, the forms of sexual relationships which have "officially," as it were, been rejected in Western thought as deviant are now being seen as the precise way to mental health and public salvation. The advocacy of "group marriage," partner exchange, homosexuality, or other forms of what was once called "perversion" goes quite beyond the old discussions of divorce or polygamy, both of which are theoretically at least based upon the retention of the family structure as a normal and basic human form.

The legal efforts to publish the books of Henry Miller are almost legendary. Miller's ultimate legal right to publish his literary product is now established almost as a direct consequence of the sexual revolution itself in which the norms of the community have become so varied. What strikes us today about such a book as *The Tropic of Capricorn,* Miller's fictional autobiography first published in Paris in 1939, is its association of hatred, mystic overtones, sex, and revolution — presently very current themes. Miller is, in a way, a true pioneer; as an example of the form this subsequent rebellion has taken he bears much study. For him, the traditional values associated with God, the family, and the

8. It is very often in the art forms that such changes are most evident, notably film, popular music, and poetry.

9. Allen Ginsberg, "Howl and Other Poems," San Francisco, City Lights Books, p. 9, in Thomas Parkinson, editor, *A Casebook on the Beat,* New York, Thomas Y. Crowell, 1961, p. 3.

10. Cf. Susan Sontag, *Against Interpretation,* New York, Delta, 1966.

nation are the very evils to be rejected. What they had formed in his personality was exactly what had to be overcome. "I had no more need of God," he wrote,

> than He had of me, and if there were one, I often said to myself, I would meet Him calmly and spit in His face . . . . The moment anything was expected or demanded of me, I balked. That was the form my independence took. I was corrupt, in other words, corrupt from the start. . . . I was against life on principle. What principle? The principle of futility.[11]

Upon this foundation of futility and independence, conceived as a release from any expected demand or obligation that could come from nature, nation, or nurture, Miller could thus reject his own history.

The two essential and constitutive elements that provide the environment of personal life are the family and the nation. To gain complete autonomy, both of these are rejected.

> My people were entirely Nordic, which is to say, *idiots*. Every wrong idea which has ever been expounded was theirs . . . . I am of the very essence of that proud, boastful Nordic people who have had the least sense of adventure but who nevertheless have scoured the earth, turned it upside down, scattered relics and ruins everywhere. Restless spirits, but not adventurous ones. Agonizing spirits, incapable of living in the present. Disgraceful cowards all of them, myself included. For there is only one great adventure and that is inward toward the self, and for that, time nor space nor even deeds matter.[12]

Time, space, and deeds — the classical signs of man — are of

---

11. Henry Miller, *The Tropic of Capricorn*, New York, Grove Press, 1961, pp. 9-10. Copyright © 1961 by Grove Press, Inc. Reprinted by permission of the publisher.

12. *Ibid.*, pp. 11-12.

the essence of contact with the past so that Miller must reject them as constitutent parts in his future.

> I have walked the streets in many countries of the world but nowhere have I felt so degraded and humiliated as in America . . . . Because in the bottom of my heart there was murder: I wanted to see America destroyed, razed from top to bottom. I wanted to see this happen purely out of vengeance, as atonement for the crimes that were committed against me and against others like me who have never been able to lift their voices and express their hatred, their rebellion, their legitimate blood lust. I was an evil product of an evil soil.[13]

The first step to finding himself, then, was the rejection of his past.

> Most of us live the greater part of our lives submerged. Certainly in my own case I can say that not until I left America did I emerge above the surface. Perhaps America had nothing to do with it, but the fact remains that I did not open my eyes until I struck Paris. And perhaps that was only because I had renounced America, renounced my past.[14]

In this context, therefore, the sexual exploits which Miller is at pains to describe become universalized means to reach a new absolute, conceived, to be sure, in sexual terms, but pleaded as a means of overcoming the alienation of the past in and through a new universal union which rejects the standards of the past.

In Miller, however, there hardly seems to be such a thing as another person, in spite of his constant concern for humanity, which, of course, is not itself, as such, a true person. Others appear to be in the category of objects, one seemingly as impersonal as the other so long as they serve to ground his search for an absolute.

13. *Ibid.*, pp. 12-13.
14. *Ibid.*, p. 49.

The other becomes a tool for something else. This feature of the sexual revolution, its failure really to confront the exigencies of the other as unique other, runs through this literature.[15] The precise scope of this tendency is to make the ethical abnormal to become the normal. "For some . . . ," Lipton writes,

> sexual experimentation is not as difficult as it is for others. As the Judaeo-Christian ethos continues to lose its grip on our educational institutions, on government, police, and the law, as its vested interests fall into decay and its die-hard defenders retire from their rear-guard positions, through defection or old-age, the new morality will show a higher and higher percentage of successful experiments, until no one will think them as experiments any longer and the vision of the new poets and myth-makers of today will finally be seen as a prophecy of the new life ways and sexways of tomorrow.[16]

What Lipton means by "experimentation," of course, involves making legal marriages optional, legalizing homosexuality, abolishing any meaning of "unnatural" acts, multiple and plural marriage, abortions on demand, and finally making all forms of mating legal when there is mutual consent. But this is not only a question of legality. Rather these varied forms of sexual life are to be experienced and promoted precisely as a *superior* way of life.

Several years ago, Lionel Trilling wrote a very illuminating essay on the Kinsey Report, the then famous American analysis of sexual practices in the United States. Trilling's analysis of the methodology and conclusions of this widely-read report are still quite pertinent to the understanding of the sexual revolution as it has developed. The Kinsey Report, Trilling pointed out, had several fundamental presuppositions. Those included a belief that

15. Cf. for a discussion of this point in another context the author's "Peace and 'Hair'," *The Month,* February 1970, pp. 102-07.

16. Lipton, p. 284.

sexuality is to be identified with its incidence or quantitative measurement.[17] This meant that frequency of sexual activity was taken to be identified with its goodness.[18] Behind this there was a studied indifference to the problem of qualitative or rational control as the primary guide for sexual activity.[19] The report also tended to identify the natural with the normal, while the normal was identified with animal rather than human behavior.

> The report has in mind both a physical normality — as suggested by its belief that under optimal conditions men should be able to achieve the orgasmic frequency of primates — and a moral normality, the acceptability, on the authority of animal behavior, of certain usually taboo practices.[20]

With this basis, the report attempted to identify the statistical incidence of what is done in the sexual sphere with what should be done so that this norm of what is done becomes itself the criterion of morality.

The criterion of what is done, therefore, became a new value or goal. "The Report has the intention of habituating its readers

17. Lionel Trilling, "The Kinsey Report," *The Liberal Imagination,* Doubleday Anchor, p. 223. Cf. Lipton, p. 11. The following remarks of Stanley Kubrick, director of the film *2001* about the sexual revolution in the next century gives some feeling for the kind of thinking that takes place in this area:

"Here again, it's pure speculation. Perhaps there will have been a reaction against present trends, and the pendulum will swing back to a kind of neo-puritanism. But it's more likely that the so-called sexual revolution, midwifed by the pill, will be extended. Through drugs, or perhaps even mechanical amplification of latent ESP functions, it may be possible to each partner to simultaneously experience the sensations of the other; or we may eventually emerge into polymorphous sexual beings, with male and female components blurring, merging, and interchanging. The potentialities for exploring new areas of sexual experience are virtually boundless." "Interview with Stanley Kubrick," *Playboy,* July 1968, p. 186.

18. Trilling, *op. cit.,* p. 224.

19. *Ibid.,* p. 229.

20. *Ibid.,* p. 227. Cf. also the discussion of the similar thesis of Robert Ardrey in the previous chapter.

to sexuality in all its manifestations; it wants to establish, as it were, *a democratic pluralism of sexuality.*" [21] This ideal, as we have already suggested earlier, sought to identify the total variety of experimental possibility with the good. In metaphysical terms, the good was equal to being where all being was simply the total statistical experience conceivable. Trilling suggested here that there was a studied effort in many American intellectual circles to make no intellectual distinctions at all in this area.

> It goes with a nearly conscious aversion from making intellectual distinctions, almost as out of the belief that all intellectual distinctions must inevitably lead to a social discrimination or exclusion. We might say that those who must explicitly assert and wish to practice the democratic virtues have taken it as their assumption that all social facts — with the exception of exclusion and economic hardships — must be accepted, not merely in the scientific sense but also in the social sense, in the sense, that is, that no judgment must be passed on them, that any conclusion drawn from them which perceives values and consequences will turn out to be "undemocratic." [22]

The upshot of this refusal to see in nature or society any norms or limits to sexuality ends up in fact by ultimately denying the reality of sex itself.[23]

The identification of sexual pluralism with a deliberate refusal to come to a critical judgment about the meaning of his pluralism can be the other side of something much more sinister, a phenomenon we have been tracing throughout this analysis. Norman Podhoretz's analysis of the sexual concepts in a writer like Jack Kerouac and the so-called "Beat Generation" of the late Fifties contains, in retrospect, some further clarity on this problem.

---

21. *Ibid.*, p. 234.
22. *Ibid.*
23. This is especially the case in which the other is either reduced to an instrument or even abolished altogether. Cf. Trilling, p. 235.

Sex has always played a very important role in Bohemianism: sleeping around was the Bohemian's most dramatic demonstration of his freedom from conventional moral standards, and a defiant denial of the idea that sex was permissible only in marriage and then only for the sake of the family. At the same time, to be "promiscuous" was to assert the validity of sexual experience in and for itself.[24]

Podhoretz sees Kerouac's use of sex not so much as a defiance such as it is in Miller or Ginsberg but as a means to form "permanent relationships." (This, of course, is the classic function of sex also.) But this seems not to involve the stability we used to associate with marriage. Rather, "what seems to be at stake here, in short, is sexual anxiety of enormous proportions . . . ."[25] This anxiety about permanent relationships shifted the nature of sexual emphasis.

Consequently, "for the new Bohemians, interracial friendships and love affairs apparently play the same role of social defiance that sex used to play for the older Bohemian circles."[26] Thus, sex comes to be used as a metaphysical and social instrument — which means, as Trilling also suggested, that sex itself was denied implicitly. There is also a latent anti-intellectualism here similar to what Trilling observed in the Kinsey Report. "I think it is legitimate to say, then, that the Beat Generation's worship of primitivism and spontaneity is more than a cover to intelligence; it arises from a pathetic poverty of feeling as well."[27]

Podhoretz's final judgment is harsh, but it does suggest a connection between this aspect of the sexual revolution and violence in the political order, an eventuality that seems to be coming about more and more.

24. Norman Podhoretz, "The Know-Nothing Bohemians," *Partisan Review,* Spring 1958, in Parkinson, p. 205.

25. *Ibid.,* p. 206.

26. *Ibid.,* p. 207.

27. *Ibid.,* p. 211.

The hipsters and hipster lovers of the Beat Generation are rebels, all right, but not against anything so sociological and historical as the middle class or capitalism or even respectability. This is the revolt of the spiritually underprivileged and the crippled of soul — young men who can't think straight and so hate anyone who can; young men who can't get outside the morass of self and so construct definitions of feeling that exclude all human beings who manage to live, even miserably, in a world of objects; young men who are burdened unto death with the specially poignant sexual anxiety that America ... seems bent on breeding, and who therefore dream of the unattainable perfect orgasm, which excuses all sexual failures in the real world.

Not long ago, Norman Mailer suggested that the rise of the hipster may represent "the first wind of a second revolution in this century, moving not forward toward action and more rational distribution, but backward toward being and the secrets of human energy." To tell the truth whenever I hear anyone talking about instinct and being and the secrets of human energy, I get nervous; next thing you know he'll be saying that violence is just fine, and then I begin wondering whether he really thinks that kicking someone in the teeth or sticking a knife between his ribs are deeds to be admired.[28]

That this later worry has, some decades later, a widespread popularity, surely goes without saying.[29]

However, the implications of Podhoretz's comment that the rebellion passes beyond those "human beings who manage, even miserably, in a world of objects" needs further comment. There are today manifold apologists who believe monogamous marriage to be out of style, that the various homo- and heterosexual ex-

28. *Ibid.*
29. Cf. the exchange between Sam Brown and Arthur M. Schlesinger Jr., in *The Endless Crisis*, New York, Simon and Schuster, 1970, pp. 283-88.

periences are to become the norm. This is the "democratic pluralism of sexuality" in which the full sexual experience includes both ethically and intellectually the participation in all the possible varieties of sex from bestiality to adultery to temporary exchanges to group arrangements to homosexuality.

Until recently, of course, certain forms of sexual experience seemed to be contradictory. And some still are — which means ultimately that reality itself necessarily imposes a limitation on man. The experience of truly monogamous marriage for a lifetime between two persons (of opposite sexes) who love one another — surely still a possibility — is metaphysically incompatible with any other simultaneous sexual experience during one lifetime. That is, homosexuality, adultery, or any other conceivable variety of sexual relationship already excludes by its very fact the life with only one woman or man. Nature itself gives a "non datur tertium" relationship, such that the choice of one style of life necessarily excludes the other.

Furthermore, to cite extreme cases, it has seemed clear that the female could not experience precisely the masculine sex experience and vice versa no matter how complementary these functions might be from nature. The recent novel, *Myra Breckenridge,* however, seems to suggest, if it can be taken seriously, that even this limitation is no longer the case. Myra Breckenridge is a man who by means of an operation and hormone implants becomes a beautiful woman, presumably having thus had the capacity to experience the reactions of both sexes in the life of one single person.

However, it is not so simple because the real theme of the book is centered on the classic homosexual frustration of power replacing love.[30] "For him (Myron, i.e., Myra as a man), to be able to take from woman her rightful pleasure — not to mention the race's instrument of generation — became a means of ex-

30. Cf. Harvey Cleckley, *The Mask of Sanity,* St. Louis, 1964.

ercising power over both sexes and, yes, even over life itself." [31]
The intellectual pretentions of such a concept are clear, that is,
the desire to control life itself. The solution to the problem of
sex, then, in this approach, involves "the polymorphous sexual
abandon in which the lives between the sexes dissolves — to the
delight of all. I suspect that this may be the only workable pattern for the future, and it is a more healthy one." [32] This is a new
state in which the very concept of sex in the traditional sense
is overthrown precisely as a means of human "delight." Such as
it is, of course, this analysis makes nonsense of the desires
and drives of what has been known, up until now, as the human
being.

Vidal also, like Henry Miller, posits a direct relation between
a new sexual order and the violent attack upon the traditional
value of the nation and the race.

> As usual I am ambivalent. On the one hand, I am in-
> tellectually devoted to the idea of the old America. I be-
> lieve in justice — I want redress for all the wrongs done.
> I want the good life — if such a thing exists — accessible to
> all. Yet emotionally, I would only be too happy to become
> world dictator, if only to fulfill my mission: the destruction of
> the last vestigial traces of traditional manhood in the race
> in order to realign the sexes, thus reducing population while
> increasing human happiness and preparing humanity for its
> next stage.[33]

Such talk of "the next stage," of course, is pretentious in the
highest degree. Population is to be reduced and traditional man-
hood abolished — phrases not unlike the pagan theories about
what to do to the subject, conquered peoples, that is, take their

31. Gore Vidal, *Myra Breckenridge*, Boston, Little, Brown, 1968, p. 92.
32. *Ibid.*, p. 109.
33. *Ibid.*, pp. 40-41.

women and kill or reduce the men to slaves. In this next state, sex no longer has any "natural" function with regard to child-bearing or even, as in the case of Myra Breckenridge, any relation to love between two distinct persons. The elimination of "the other" from the practice and concept of love removes its pos-sibility. The world of the self and self-power is all that is left.

The fundamental issue of our time, then, concerns the validity of the structures of man as he has evolved from nature in the course of the ages. Has man come to be what and as he is by mere chance? Even worse, perhaps, as many are beginning to suggest, man may be quite badly made by natural evolution, a mistake and an error like other discarded creatures of evolution.[34] Professor P. B. Medawar has warned, "that nature does not know best; that genetical evolution, if we choose to look at it liverishly instead of with fatuous good humor, is a story of waste, makeshift, compromise, and blunder."[35] On the other hand, is human reality the result of something in the order of design and plan, as Aristotle had held? Is the admitted uniqueness of man in nature, his heterosexual structure, his mind, his hands, is this merely an aggrandizement or alienation or is it central and paramount, perhaps the very meaning of the cosmos itself?[36] Though, in strict logic, this should not necessarily be the case, it is frequently assumed today that man's growing capacity to

34. For two surprising views of this kind of modernized "original sin" theory, cf. Arthur Koestler, "The Urge to Self-Destruction," *Chemistry in Britain*, 4 April 1970; Max Tishler, "To Awaken the Virtue of a Careless Age," *Chemical and Engineering News*, 9 March 1970, pp. 80-82.

35. P. B. Medawar, *The Future of Man*, New York, Basic Books, 1959, p. 100.

36. The essence of classic Aristotelian thought follows this latter type of reasoning, as does that of Teilhard de Chardin. This is why the effort of the French philosopher Jacques Monod to eliminate "scientifically" order and priority in nature must attack all theories from Christianity to Marx which are founded upon the uniqueness and purposefulness of man. Cf. J. Monod, *Il Caso e La Necessità*, trans., italiana, S. Busi, Milano, Mondadori, 1970.

understand and manipulate the physical universe makes any problem about the unity and order of that plan outside man irrelevant. We have already seen something of how ecological sciences and the anti-rational elements in our revolutionary movements are more and more rejecting this connection between nature and intelligence.

The fact that man is grasping laws that he did not institute should not, however, lead us to the conclusion that these laws are now of man's own making, laws which because of their human comprehension require no further explanation outside the fact that man now knows them. Yet, there is no doubt an underlying mood, perhaps less popular today than it was even a few years ago, which would assume that the discovery of the physical processes of nature, their reproduction by human artifacts, eliminates any need of further philosophical analysis. Indeed, a whole ethic and philosophy are based upon this assumption that the growth of human knowing and technique eradicates the need of a further criterion. That this view, intended to elevate man, really lowers him is suggested by the fact that it closes him in a reality no broader than himself, in the belief that this must be all that there is. The human comes to be identified with the all.

Nevertheless, the "structure" of man has become problematic because genetic and biological sciences especially have opened up the practical possibility of a basic altering of the human experience and physical form into a shape outside of, if not contrary to, the traditional notes that have defined the normal being of man. Science, in this sense, is beginning to make possible concrete visions of the ethical chaos of our times. Up until this generation, man has never had to worry about what he would be on the physical side of his being since that was supposedly determined by the exigencies of creation, environment, or natural selection. We are rapidly coming to recognize, however, that man can be made radically otherwise. And it is frequently suggested that because man can be otherwise, he should be. It is in the exposition and analysis of these concrete proposals about potential changes in man that we can most clearly observe the profundity of the changes in modern thought.

Even further, the real evils of man are more and more believed to be rooted precisely in the double sexual, family-oriented, politically disposed condition of man. There is a growing school of thought — logically connected with the theories of population control and technological capacity — which believes that man would be improved by removing the child-bearing aspect of human life from the arbitrariness of individual human couples. "An absolute check will require not only that birth control techniques be made available," Professor Hermann Muller wrote,

> but also that large masses of people execute an about face in their attitude toward having children. They must recognize that to have or not to have children, and how many, should be determined primarily by the interests of the children themselves — that is, the next and subsequent generations. If this change in outlook is effected —as it must be sooner or later — it is a relatively short step to the realization that *the inborn equipment of the children also counts mightily in their well-being and opportunity for happiness.*[37]

37. Hermann Muller, "The Guidance of Human Evolution," *The Evolution of Man,* Sol Tax, editor, Chicago, University of Chicago Press, Vol. II, p. 438.
Dobzhansky gives the following summary of Muller's thesis:
"It is, however, perfectly imaginable that techniques may be invented to dispense with sexual reproduction altogether, by implanting nuclei of body (somatic) cells into enucleated eggs and making them develop without fertilization (parthenogenetically).
Suppose then that we have available body cells of truly great men and women, preserved in special cultures in a deep-frozen condition, and the techniques are available to make these cells develop into whole organisms. One could at any time bring into the world any number of persons who would resemble the respective donors of the cells as much as if these donors had identical twin brothers or sisters. The limit would be to select the ideal man or the ideal woman, and to have the entire population of the world, the whole of mankind carry this genotype. All

This, of course, is but a sophisticated way of saying that the genetic welfare of future generations must become the primary reproductive norm, not the real human beings that are in fact produced by nature. And genetic quality may well eventually exclude the very idea of human parents, or the right of a man to marry any woman of his choice for the purpose of having their own children. The logic of subsequent generations as the ethical norm for deciding who or how children should be allowed to come to be must eventually come to the conclusion that having children is something much too important to be left to "mere" human couples. The more radical exponents of this line of thought even wonder whether heterosexuality itself is really necessary or even advantageous.[38]

The idea of a radical separation between sexuality and reproduction seems, at first sight, to be a carry over from science fiction. Yet, as we are beginning to see, this is what lies behind much of the logic of modern sexual and birth control theory. The idea that sex and reproduction necessarily go together, then, is not, intellectually, merely a puritan hang-over or a Catholic fetish, but rather something that brings into question the very being of man as we have historically known him when it is denied. Thus, what is beginning to be proposed is that these two things do not belong together. As seems clear, it is rather the proponents of genetic control over the human race who are the quickest to grasp that they must break the connection of sex and reproduction to gain full control over man's future.

---

men (or all women — one could, if desired, have individuals of one sex only) would then be born not only equal but indeed genetically alike," in T. Dobzhansky, *Mankind Evolving*, Yale University Press, 1962, p. 329. Cf. H. J. Muller, "Control by Choice of Gene Cells," *Current*, January 1962, pp. 53-58.

The anti-democratic, elitist nature of this thesis should not be passed over, nor its implied denigration of the rights of the ordinary man.

38. Cf. Gordon Rattray Taylor, *The Biological Time-Bomb*, New York, World, 1968, p. 40ff.

Those groups, then, religious and secular, which might be expected in some sense to rise to the defense of human sexuality and the human family as something more than mere evolutionary accidents are so chaotically dispersed over the minor problem of the technicalities of contraception that they are yielding the field by default. "Again, the discovery of oral contraceptives is merely the beginning of a new world of expertise in the control of the reproductive problems," Gordon Rattray Taylor has rightly observed, "and the controversies which have raged about the use of such pills will soon be lost in the thunder of more desperate battles." [39] The more desperate battles are already upon us. And we are being more and more told that man can have his sex to play with and enjoy as much as he likes; the only thing he must give up is reproduction for the good of subsequent generations, together with children in his own image. All this is to be done in the name of some more genetically perfect form.

The development of scientific thought is, as we have suggested earlier, related to the Judaeo-Christian idea of the relation between man and nature, in the idea that God and nature proceed according to law. In this sense, Christianity and science were seen as actually guilty for our so-called ecological crisis in recent years. On the other hand, there is a segment of scientific thought — perhaps up until recently the more powerful one — which strove to disassociate itself from the Christian implications while, at the same time, seeking to retain the idea that man is the irreducible center of reality. The basis of this second view is the presumed scientific and technical capacity of man to eliminate from nature any criterion of finality, any value or norm other than man. With the need of God or a First Mover removed, the human intelligence comes almost necessarily to replace the God of the Christians or nature itself as the crux of the ethical universe.[40] Human superiority in the world is based on man's

39. Taylor, p. 12.
40. Cf. Ernest Cassirer, *An Essay on Man*, Doubleday Anchor, 1944,

capacity to use nature creatively whereas nature herself merely repeats, seemingly, without consciously knowing. Thus, nature is reduced to human intelligence so that nothing becomes scientifically "real" unless it can be reproduced and therefore dominated. It is only recently that man himself is coming to be seen as falling likewise into this category of artificially reproducible beings.

The history of how this development occurred is essential to an understanding of the modern world.[41] It involves a long line of thought which leads from Aristotle, to the post-Aristotelians, to Augustine, the Scholastics, to Roger Bacon, the revival of post-Aristotelian thought in the seventeenth and eighteenth centuries, to Machiavelli, Descartes, Hume, Kant, Feuerbach, Marx, and Darwin. The net effect of this development was to remove teleology from nature so that man was no longer a certain kind of being established in his uniqueness by what lay beyond nature itself.

But if nature no longer provides a reason for man being unique and prior in nature itself, then, a substitute must be found to shore up the loss of the human position. At first, this basis was believed to be found in the intellect's capacity to know and to change reality. But if man has no intrinsic finality, if he along with all the rest of nature, can be otherwise than he is, then there is likewise no fundamental reason for man to remain being man when a way is discovered to make him into something else. The very reason for human uniqueness in the world turns out to be a reason for changing man into something else, something hopefully higher than he was found to be in nature. Classical thought, to be sure, believed man to be somehow higher than his own natural claims might warrant. But the modern conclusion arrives not at a positive position of defending man as he is

---

Chapter I; Charles N. R. McCoy, *The Structure of Political Thought,* New York, McGraw-Hill, 1963; also the author's "The Significance of Post-Aristotelian Thought in Political Theory," *Cithara,* November 1963.

41. Cf. McCoy.

received from nature as somehow a higher creature, but at the pragmatic possibility of changing him into something else. The necessity for this conclusion which radically questions the very being of man has escaped many historians of science and society who still cling to the post-Marxian idea that the human intelligence's capacity gives it the absolute right to control and therefore to change all reality it can comprehend into the human freed from norms. In short, without some more adequate theory about the human, there is no ability to distinguish between deformity and normalcy.

The view that man's capacity to base his uniqueness on his technique is, in a sense, radically anti-historical because history cannot be a source of knowledge about what man is or what he can become. Rightly enough, this elimination of history is believed to remove effectively the claims of religion to influence this discussion since religion, more especially Christianity, is basically historical, if, in fact, along with Judaism, it did not invent the very notion of history. "So we must now learn to play God," Professor Edmund Leach, the noted English anthropologist, has written,

in the moral as well as in the creative or destructive sense. To do this effectively, we shall have to educate our children in quite a different way. In the past, education has always been designed to inculcate a respect for the wisdom and experience of the older generation, whose members have been credited with an intuitive understanding of the wishes of an omniscient God. From this point of view, the dogmas of religion represent the sum of our historical experience. So long as it appeared that "natural law" was external and unalterable — except by God — it was quite sensible to use history in this way as a guide to virtue. But in our changed circumstances, when we ourselves can alter all the ground rules of the game, excessive deference to established authority could well be an invitation

to disaster . . . . We ourselves have to decide what is sin and
what is virtue . . . .[42]

This removal of history, it is to be noted, is what forces science
to take up the moral question of who is to live or not live.[43] And
this is to be decided on criteria not based upon the traditional
commitment to life.[44]

42. Edmund Leach, "We Scientists Have the Right to Play God,"
The Saturday Evening Post, 16 November 1968, p. 20. Reprinted with
permission of *The Saturday Evening Post* © 1968 The Curtis Publishing
Co. For a brilliant discussion on the relation of history to Christian theology
and modern thought, cf. O. Cullmann, *Christ and Time,* Philadelphia,
Westminster, 1950.

43. Leach, p. 20.

44. Professor Hans Jonas has, in writing about the problems of human
experimentation, clearly spelled out the implications of these problems:

"The patient must be absolutely sure that his doctor does not become
his executioner, and that no definition authorizes him ever to become one.
His right to this certainty is absolute, so is his right to his own body
with all its organs. Absolute respect for these rights violates no one else's
rights, for no one has the right to another's body. Speaking in still another
religious vein: The expiring moments should be watched over with piety
and be safe from exploitation . . . .

Let us not forget that progress is an optional goal, not an unconditional
commitment, and that its tempo in particular, compulsive as it may
become, has nothing sacred about it. Let us also remember that a slower
progress in the conquest of disease would not threaten society, grievous
as it is to those who have to deplore that their particular disease be not
yet conquered, but that society would indeed be threatened by the erosion
of those moral values whose loss, possibly caused by too ruthless a
pursuit of scientific progress, would make its most dazzling triumphs
not worth having. Let us finally remember that it cannot be the aim of
progress to abolish the lot of mortality. Of some ill or other, each of
us will die. Our mortal condition is upon us with its harshness but also
its wisdom — because without it there would not be the eternally renewed
promise of the freshness, immediacy, and eagerness of youth; nor, without
it, would there be for any of us the incentive to number our days and
make them count, with all our striving to wrest from our mortality what
we can, we should bear its burden with patience and dignity." Hans Jonas,
"Philosophical Reflections on Experimenting with Human Subjects,"
Daedalus, Spring 1969, p. 245. Reprinted by permission from *Daedalus,*
Journal of the American Academy of Arts and Sciences, Boston, Mass.,
Vol. 98, No. 2.

Professor J. Bronowski has endeavored to give this notion of a scientific humanist ethic a more firm, even historical basis. In order to do this, Bronowski must retain the Christian notion of the uniqueness of man without reverting to the eco-logical-naturalist thesis of man as purely a part of evolved nature. The humanist thesis which, according to Bronowski, must join to science if we are to preserve mankind, is "anti-authoritarian" so that it must only be based on a free assent to a self-evident truth.[45] The history of science has resulted in an elevation of man in the humanist direction. "In humanism, man is all things: he is both the expression and the master of creation . . . the first principle of humanism is that the creation is fulfilled in human experience." [46] The crucial question, then, is how to join this humanist priority to science.

The manner in which these two movements joined in the past is important. It was commonly assumed that the Copernican revolution in astronomy has displaced man from his traditional superiority in nature. But, as Professor Bronowski continues, this was not at all the case. On the contrary, the new astronomy proved that the same laws that ruled the heavens also ruled the earth so that in learning the laws of earth, man learned the laws of the universe at the same time.[47] It was the history of magic that provided the clue whereby science became human in a new way.

Magic was, first of all, ". . . a system of devices for making nature obey men." [48] Magic, however, depended upon a belief in an animistic nature and the possibility of man gaining control over this world spirit so that man could control natural events by controlling this spirit. Through da Vinci especially, magic gradually

45. J. Bronowski, "Science as a Humanistic Discipline," *The Bulletin of the Atomic Scientists,* October 1968, p. 34. For a further discussion of the Bronowski thesis, cf. the author's "The Urgency and the Waiting," *World Justice,* #4, 1969-70, pp. 435-59.
46. Bronowski, *op. cit.,* p. 34.
47. *Ibid.*
48. *Ibid.,* p. 37.

began to shift from an occult science to a learning of the natural powers that control the universe. Nature, it was learned, was not a world spirit, but had laws and man could know them. But this destruction of belief in magic through a grasp of the laws of nature had the result of reducing man. "Man, the power of mind, is no longer primary, and nature, the reach of law, is no longer secondary in the order of our thought, as they were when humanism began." [49] At first sight, this has brought about a "crisis of self-confidence" which has apparently undermined the inherited Christian-humanist belief in the primacy of man.

How can this humanist priority be regained? Only by being loyal to the facts of nature which show that man does have unique capacities.[50] This uniqueness is not founded on a theory of religion but apparently on scientific observation. "Science . . . has to transmit this sense of uniqueness, and to found it on the order of nature and not on the primacy of man." [51] In classical Aristotelian thought, it is well to recall here, man's uniqueness was established precisely because he was able to transcend the repetitive order of nature. It was because he was not merely a part of nature that nature was subject to him, to his control.

For Bronowski, however, man's observed capacity to symbolize, to see the consequences of his acts is merely a result of a natural fact so that the dignity and value of man are to be created by him:

> We are the creatures who have to create values in order to elucidate our own conduct and to learn from it so that we can direct it into the future. The humanist reality is that man is guided by values and that he creates them for himself. This is the hard discipline which it now falls *to science to teach to a world that has lost the comfort of being sustained by any absolute principles.*[52]

49. *Ibid.,* p. 38.
50. *Ibid.,* p. 37.
51. *Ibid.,* p. 38.
52. *Ibid.*

But this attempt to ground man in something other than "the comfort of absolute principles" is itself bound to failure for man can both change and destroy what is, in fact, human. The "self-created" values are still self-created even when they are monstrous distortions of the human.

There is no way to contemplate more graphically the tenuousness of the theory Bronowski proposes for grounding the human without a belief in man that is somehow beyond his own making than to continue to examine, now from a scientific rather than literary viewpoint, the concrete, proposed experiments designed to "improve" man. We shall see that every essential note that is held to be a part of the very structure of man is under question. Furthermore, there appears to be no reason why most of these proposals cannot be effected in reality if someone should want to do so. Whether they will or not come into being is to be the result of choice and understanding from now on, not the result of lack of technique and facility which have protected much of the human so far.

If we attempt to list the characteristics thought historically to compose the human being as a distinct being in nature, we should have to include the following:

1) man is in some basic sense different from the animals.

2) each individual is unique and irrepeatable.

3) man is two sexed, male and female, existing in approximately the same proportions.

4) human offspring are begotten by a union of a human male and a human female, according to a natural process wherein gestation takes place in the female womb, birth occuring about nine months after conception.

5) the human family, centered on the human parents with a right and a capacity to produce their own children, is the locus in which the child is nurtured and raised to maturity.

6) virtue and vice are the results of free will choice and knowledge.

7) man can attain full human perfection in his earthly aspect only in a political community.

8) man is mortal, subject to sickness and eventual death.

9) man's basic form and dignity to be man are not created by man.

When we examine the current literature in genetics, biology and medicine, we discover that each of these elements is questioned on the grounds that the man who has in fact evolved from nature is, supposedly, inferior and to be ethically and even physically eliminated in favor of a "better being." [53]

The only way to retain man as we know him is, therefore, through a retention of the relationship between sex and reproduction. Intellectually, this is the crucial area which, if not valid, allows each of the proposed changes to follow logically and necessarily. In this way, we create a new and dangerous form of the "new Adam," the new man. It is the theoretical and practical separation of these functions which ultimately allows the new genetic theories to come into being. This is why a belief in man as he is historically known is bound up with an intrinsic relation between man and reproduction. "The procedure of sexual enjoyment," Gordon Rattray Taylor correctly has observed,

> has finally become wholly divorceable from the procedure of procreation. Contraception can be used to prevent pro-

53. Besides the literature cited in this chapter, the following works might be mentioned:

Jean Rostand, *Can Man Be Modified?* New York, Basic Books, 1959; *Control of Human Heredity and Evolution,* T. Sonneborn, editor, Macmillan; *Biological Aspects of Social Problems,* Meade and Parks, editors, New York, Plenum, 1965.

For a calm discussion of how feasible many of these genetic proposals are in practice, cf. Bernard D. Davis, "Prospects for Genetic Intervention in Man," *Science,* 18 December 1970, pp. 1279-83.

creation when the sexual act is preferred, while artificial insemination and artificial inovulation, separately or together, can be used to bring about procreation without the occurrence of the sexual act. Thus, it becomes possible to introduce a eugenic policy without interfering in people's choice of mate or marital partner.[54]

This proposed eugenic policy, needless to say, would have one slight drawback from a more historical point of view — that is, one's children would not really be one's own, which is what the exclusiveness of the sexual act between known, committed partners was about in the first place.

Once a belief in the validity of the sexual act as a direct relation between living partners designed to produce and foster a known family is given up, not only does the concept of "parenthood" rapidly disappear, not to mention the very notions of brother to a brother and sister to a sister, but even the very idea of finite, family life. "Hitherto ... it has been usual for a child to be born of two parents of differing sex, both of whom were alive at the time of his/her conception," Professor Taylor continues,

such tedious limitations are rapidly disappearing with unforeseeable consequences for marriage and the family as we know it. Thanks to techniques for storing the male seed,

54. Taylor, *op. cit.*, p. 158.
"Furthermore, it is difficult to see why the sterilized individuals should be held to monogamy — or even why those adjudged unsuitable to rear children should trouble to maintain any domestic life at all. The family is already being eroded by the inventions of the school and state, and this might be its *coup de grace*.
As Dr. Robert S. Morison of Cornell puts it: 'Once sex and reproduction are separated, society will have to struggle with ... defining the nature of interpersonal relationships which have no social point ... and seek new ways to insure reasonable care for infants and children in an emotional atmosphere which lacks biological reinforcement ....' The language is a bit abstract but the point is a strong one." Taylor, p. 179.

it is already the case that a child may be conceived long after the death of the father and a woman might bear a child to her great-grandfather one day. Indeed, research now in hand may make it possible for a woman to bear a child without male intervention, or even for a child to be born without the comfort of a maternal womb. The parents, if any, may be able to specify the sex of the child in advance, and even change it . . . . In the field of aging, gerontologists foresee both an extension of the life span and the preservation of a degree of youthful vigor into old age. Some even contemplate the possibility of immortality.[55]

What we should note in passing is that the hope for a this-world immortality, a generation that does not pass away, is also a generation that necessarily eliminates sex as a reproducing agent since immortality really implies the need of no more children.[56]

Yet, there are more profound philosophical and theological overtones within these intimations to immortality. The frankest and most forthright statement of the proposed alterations in man are those of Joshua Lederberg. In a significant phrase, at least from the viewpoint of the history of modern thought, Professor Lederberg speaks "about the criteria for the 'good man' which is the aim of eugenic policy."[57] The importance of this

55. *Ibid.,* p. 11. Cf. also George B. Leonard, "Why We Need a New Sexuality," *Look,* January 13, 1970, p. 54.
56. Cf. Karl Rahner, "Experiment: Man," in *Science and Faith in the 21st Century,* D. Brophy, editor, New York, Paulist, 1968, pp. 11-38. This whole book is pertinent to this topic.
57. Joshua Lederberg, "Experimental Genetics and Human Evolution," in *Beyond Left and Right,* R. Kostelanetz, editor, New York, William Morrow, 1968, p. 180. (This essay can also be found in *The American Naturalist,* 1966; and in *The Bulletin of the Atomic Scientists,* October 1966). For a specific critique of the Lederberg thesis, cf. Paul Ramsey, in *Who Shall Live?* Philadelphia, Fortress Press, 1970. Cf. Henry Winthrop, "L'avenir de la révolution sexuelle," *Diogène,* No 70, Avril-Juin, 1970, pp. 65-94; Robert Francoeur, *Utopian Motherhood; New Trends in Human Reproduction,* New York, Doubleday, 1970.

approach can hardly be overemphasized for it is nothing less than the abandonment of the idea of "the good man" as the product of his free will choices about his given mortal, human life. The good man is conceived not as the product of moral choices taken personally by him in the companionship of his fellow man but of genetic control exercised by science during the process of his coming to be.

What does this proposed 'good man' look like? Lederberg is frank in recognizing much more clearly than Bronowski that traditional humanist presuppositions cannot stand in the light of the new biology shorn of absolute principles. "It is very difficult to see how we can reconcile any aggressive negative eugenic program with humanistic aspirations for individual self-expression and the approbation of diversity." [58] The problems do not arise so much from the use of genetic procedures to cure or prevent disease or deformities. This is what justifies this sort of experimentation.[59] But massive transplantations and the problem of the preservation of life by highly technological means beyond all hope of recovery create serious problems. "Inevitably, biological knowledge weighs many human beings with personal responsibility for decisions that were once relegated to Divine Providence." [60] Life, the form of life, and the time and moment of death, then, come ever more into the frail hands of men.

Such godlike choices, moreover, can involve three basic decisions that change man radically. In our times, it is becoming possible to eliminate sexual differences, to mix animal and human chromosomes, and to fuse animal and human parts so

58. Lederberg, *op. cit.*, p. 182.
59. *Ibid.*, p. 183.
60. *Ibid.*, p. 184.
"If the world will only listen, they (biological revolutionaries) know how to put us on the high road to salvation. What exactly does their brand of salvation entail? Perhaps the most illuminating way to put the matter is that their ideal is the manufacture of man." Donald Fleming, "On Living in a Biological Revolution," *The Atlantic,* February 1969, p. 15.

that the resultant chimera is a being somewhere in between man and beast. Finally, it may be possible to produce the human species by "vegetative propagation" so that the sexual distinction becomes wholly unnecessary. These proposals and possibilities, according to Lederberg, deserve serious discussion. "Half the beneficiaries of eugenic design will be women. Will their creativity and happiness be augmented in a genotype that recombines XX and a set of male-oriented autonomes? Or shall we bypass the dimorphism and evolve a race where this does not matter?" [61] It can be seen that the thesis of *Myra Breckenridge,* no matter how absurd in concept, has its counterpart in scientific circles.

Just as a single sex instead of two may be superior for this new being and for the 'good life' of man, so for economic or cultural reasons we may find it useful to produce on a mass scale beings half way between man and animals to do our work or recreation for us. "Human nuclei, and individual chromosomes and genes of the karo-type, will also be recombined with cells of animal species —extracorporeal gestation would merely accelerate these experiments." The human, thus, will come to mean what we feel to be human. "Pragmatically, the legal privileges of humanity will remain with objects that look enough like men to grip their consciences, and whose nurture does not cost too much." [62] With some historical perspective, this seems to be a most frightening and paradoxical conclusion — the human is only that which others are willing to recognize, provided it does not cost too much.

By far the most fascinating proposal, however, is simply that we directly reproduce offspring on the same identical patterns as the existing ones and that any sexual reproduction in the traditional sense be reserved to a few privileged souls for breeding and experimental purposes.[63] There is no sense, we are told, in sub-

61. Lederberg, *op. cit.,* p. 188.
62. *Ibid.,* p. 193.
63. *Ibid.,* p. 195.

jecting offspring to the recombinations implied by heterosexual reproduction. "If a superior individual (and presumably then genotype) is identified, why not copy it directly, rather than suffer all the risks of recombinational disruption, including those of sex . . . ? Why not be sure of an exact copy of yourself rather than risk a homozygous segregant; or at worst copy your spouse and allow some degree of biological parenthood." [64] The very ideas of chance and newness and surprise are thus removed from this system. The very essence of historical reality, that it could never be exactly the same, is thus reduced to an utter boredom of the self without even the variety of another.

In this sense, then, sexual reproduction if it is to be had at all would only be for the few. Needless to say, the definition of who exactly are to be these "superior individuals" who could have this privilege has totalitarian overtones of the clearest type. "Leave sexual reproduction for experimental purposes; when a suitable type is ascertained, take care to maintain it by clonal propagation." [65] The limits of individual mortality might thus be bridged as we could reproduce an identical being in each time period and as many of the same individuals as we wanted. "From a strictly biological standpoint, tempered clonality could allow the best of both worlds — we would at least enjoy being able to observe the experiment of discovering whether a second Einstein would outdo the first one." [66] This last observation is a most graphic one, for the new production of Einstein or of any individual, is not the result of sexual love opening a wholly new adventure on the part of human parents but a scientific initiative to see if one identical genetic structure could compete with itself for scholarly amusement and scientific progress. Unique-

64. *Ibid.,* p. 191.
65. *Ibid.,* (Clonal propagation, i.e., after the manner of shoots of vegetables.)
66. *Ibid.,* p. 192.

ness in time and space, individuality itself, become absurd.

In any case, there should be no doubt about the serious intellectual consequences of such trends of scientific thought. Alfred Rosenfeld has further spelled out the issue. The separation of sex and reproduction argues necessarily the end of the institutions of marriage and the family.[67] Lederberg has seen even more clearly that it means also the end of sex itself. "Children may routinely be born of geographically separated or even long dead parents," Rosenfeld continues. "Virgin births may become relatively common, women may give birth to other women's children, romance and genetics may finally be separated, and a few famed men may be called upon to father thousands of babies." [68] The right of a man and a woman to marry, then, their right to beget and raise children who are the direct result of their relationship and life is fundamentally challenged by any theory that separates sex and reproduction. The idea that a new human life should be achieved in some other way is not just an alternative proposal, but a contradiction to the reality man has lived and has been given.

"If the biological foundations of present day morality are removed," Rosenfeld continues, "cannot it be logically argued that this morality, every last time-honored shred of it, has become nothing but a useless anachronism?" [69] The very structure of human love is undermined when sex has no serious results in the visible world, when the relation of the sexual act and human reproduction need not be maintained. "With old fears replaced by new freedoms, do the foundations of fidelity become an outmoded concept? And if sex outside the marriage bed is OK, what happens to marriage itself? Do we marry for love, companionship, security? And are these lasting?" Rosenfeld's imaginary fancy must represent, along with some of the other similar proposals we have

67. Albert Rosenfeld, "The Second Genesis," *Life,* 7 July 1969, p. 33.
68. *Ibid.,* p. 34.
69. *Ibid.,* p. 38.

seen earlier, one of the lowest depths to which the human spirit
has sunk in recent years:

> A man in our time, feeling overburdened by his confusions
> and responsibilities, might see distinct advantages in the more
> carefree kind of world that the new biology could make fea-
> sible. He might even envy his imaginary counterpart in one
> of the possible societies of the not-too-far-off future — a man
> grown in vitro, say, and raised in a state nursery. Such a
> man, it is true, might never know who his genetic parents were,
> nor would he have any brothers or sisters he could call his
> own. On the other hand, if he considered all men his brothers,
> what need would he have for a few specifically designated sib-
> lings who happen to be born in the same household? Think
> how carefree he might be: no parents to feel guilty about
> neglecting, no parental responsibilities of his own, no mar-
> riage partner to whom he owes fidelity, free to play, work,
> create, pursue his own pleasures. In our current circumstances,
> the absence of a loved one saddens us, and death brings terrible
> grief. Think how easily the tears could be wiped away if
> there were no single "loved one" to miss that much — or if
> that loved one were readily replaceable by any of several
> others.
> And yet if you (the hypothetical in vitro man) did not miss
> anyone very much, neither would anyone miss you very much.
> Your absence would cause little sadness, your death little
> grief. You too would be readily replaceable.
> A man needs to be needed. Who, in this new era, would
> need you? Would your mortality not weigh upon you even
> more heavily, though your life span were doubled or tripled?[70]

It would be difficult to portray more vividly what mankind has

70. *Ibid.,* p. 44.

at stake in retaining the being that he is. We are being offered replaceable man with no one to blame for his existence, no one to love it either, no one to worry about his uniqueness and passing in this world —this is the final comfort we are offered by our current scientific movements which retain no absolute principles for retaining the mortality and finiteness of men.

Again we see that a slight deviation can result in a monstrous error. It seems neutral and harmless, the idea that man and his sexuality are to be separated, even for a moment, ever so slightly. Yet thought itself, it would seem, thinks out the consequences in a rigorous logic.[71] The real result is the destruction of the human itself in some fundamental fashion unless it is understood what the issues for man really are. The reconstruction and improvement of man are indeed possible. The scientists and literati who could gain control of state genetic policy could, if some of their theories are applied, destroy the traditional home of man in the name of the good genetic life.

The tragedy, then, is how few seem to be aware of where the human rights and dignities and happinesses of the ordinary man lie and why they must be understood and protected. They will no longer, as in the past, be safeguarded by ignorance and nature, only by will and reason. Who can resist pointing out to the men of our time that their pursuit of sex is ending up by eliminating first their children, then their sex itself? This result would be funny, were it not so sad. And we must recognize that this elimination of family and sex is no aberrant or illogical thing but the direct intellectual consequences of the most fashionable and popular sexual, abortion, and family planning theories. Without faith in the man that nature and history has given to us, it is more and more impossible to save him.

---

71. This is why ignorance of a potential development is not enough to guarantee in the long run that it will not happen. What there must be is real understanding of the trends and issues involved in historical perspective.

The problem of the sexual and genetic revolutions, therefore, is one of highly serious proportions for mankind. There is a great and firm relationship between the denial of a "natural" order or standard structure in man which has created or evolved him as he is, a norm discovered by his intelligence but not created by it and the subsequent elimination of family and sex altogether. The supreme irony of the sexual revolution, to repeat, is the abolition of sex as the human race has known it. When Karl Marx wrote that he wanted all natural values overturned precisely as a means to replace the "natural" with the "human," he wrote more wisely than he realized. For it is now becoming well within the possibility of man's capacity to replace sex itself as it is received from nature. Indeed the ecological schools hold that it is nature as well as technology that demands this. All this is the result of the refusal to accept the natural intentions of sex as it relates to the child and to the spouses. The responsibility of choosing one's spouse to found a real family, to create something "new" in the world is to be taken from the majority of men in the name of both sexes — all forms of sexual activity are licit and scientific — and of science — children are to be produced scientifically for the genetic good of the race.

Thus, the multiplication of sexual partners to include hetero- and homosexual varieties of all types in a casual frequency has its initial and theoretic justification, according to recent theorists, in proposing to man to experience in himself the whole gamut of reality provided by the category of sex as a way to dominate and control the source of life itself. In this sense, it has metaphysical and theological implications in seeking to share all being, in performing the precise function of "divine Providence," as Lederberg has correctly seen. But the very effort to achieve this goal in physical experience ends up, as we have seen, in a denial of sex.

The intellectual refusal or intellectual inability to judge that sex does have a natural finality in man which is one of the constituent parts of his being a man becomes thus the major cause for the disappearance of sex itself. The confusion of sexual activity, its variety and frequency in the experimental order, with love, makes love and therefore sex impossible. When the full variety and frequency of sexual activity is seen to be a means to a new freedom, a new Adam, undertaken directly contrary to the moral structure of the past, to the standard of sexual purpose in nature, then the purpose of this new act is precisely to defy nature's form and thereby to set up man's own sphere as something under his own power, to create another form of life somehow superior to the model of nature.

But sex and its natural function in these contexts becomes scientifically unnecessary, as we have suggested. Thus, without an intellectual appreciation of sex as itself having natural ends which cannot be violated without an attack on the meaning of man himself, there is no man as we have known him, as he has come from nature and history. We now have the scientific power, ecological will and intellectual temptation to remove sex itself from man.

A "democratic pluralism of sexuality," a rebellion against the implications of monogamy in love and family, the "polymorphous sexual abandon," all end up by destroying the meaning of sex even on the biological and psychic levels. The scientists are merely carrying out what our contemporary moral standards suggest to their logical conclusions. This is why the sexual revolution in its fundamental implications is anti-intellectual with regard to the natural intentions of nature, for it is a refusal to admit that what has made man to be the way he is has made him greater than any of the alternatives that we have seen.

There is an intelligence at work beyond the genius of human intelligence. But simultaneously, the refusal to admit the normative value of man creates a gigantic intellectual reaction which seeks to replace God who formed man to be a certain kind of being sexually with a man whose sexual experience has no natural limits or purpose. But when this result is finally achieved, not only is sex not necessary with regard to children, it is not necessary at all. The paradox is that the God of nature is the God of sex. Intellectually, when man seeks to change this natural order to his own image, he can do everything God can do, everything that is, but keep sex as a part of his human experience.

THE CONFUSION OF FOOD AND POPULATION

4 What most attracts attention in any discussion of population is not the theoretical presuppositions relating to its growth or decline, nor its relation to abortion or genetic control, but rather the widely discussed view that immediate population control by whatever means is the *only* alternative to starvation. It is important to understand something of the style of thought that reaches this conclusion and to put it into the context of wider disciplines and concepts of which it seems chronically unaware. What we wish to suggest here is that "starvation" on a mass scale is undoubtedly "possible," but that this "possibility," should it eventuate, would be the result of a choice, social and political, *not* to make starvation unnecessary and not to understand the forces that have already surpassed the narrow-based thinking that arrives at the food-population dilemma.[1]

Behind almost every proposal for abortion or genetic control lies a more palatable consideration which somehow tries to make such extreme measures seem logical and necessary. Essentially, some form of this argument is put forward: "unless we limit our numbers, we shall eventually, usually sooner than later, starve or die of stress."[2] After the 1969 Meeting of the American Association for the Advancement of Science, under the headline, "Doom Forecast by Year 2000," we read the following summary:

> Eventually, in fact, we may have to "fall back on a new 'stone age' in which ordinary rock is crushed to extract its

1. "For one thing, our system of modern communications, effective as it is as an instrument of public education, is producing a dangerous side effect. I believe too many people, bombarded daily by the mass media's pessimistic and disheartening emphasis on such subjects as pollution, poverty, and problems of controlling exploding population and explosive political and military power, are falling victim to negativism and despair. Filled with a mixture of shocking facts and gloomy forecasts, they are too readily accepting the belief that we cannot or will not turn the tide of our mounting problems. They see only disaster ahead . . . .

Physically we are better equipped than at any time in human history to resolve these problems and realize many of man's age-old dreams. And our awareness of our problems and our knowledge of the urgency with which we must deal with them are also positive factors that are going to work in our favor despite the current pessimism they create." Glenn T. Seaborg, Chairman, U.S. Atomic Energy Commission, "Science, Technology, and the Citizen," *Vital Speeches*, 15 October 1969, p. 6.

2. "A finite world can support only a finite population . . . . No technical solution can rescue us from the misery of overpopulation. Freedom to breed will bring ruin to all. At the moment, to avoid hard decisions many of us are tempted to propagandize for conscience and responsible parenthood. The temptation must be resisted, because an appeal to independently acting consciences selects for the disappearance of all conscience in the long run, and an increase in anxiety in the short.

The only way we can preserve and nurture other and more precious freedoms is by relinquishing the freedom to breed, and that very soon." Garrett Hardin, "The Tragedy of the Commons," in *The Environmental Handbook*, Garrett de Bell, editor, New York, Ballantine, 1970, pp. 33, 49.

metallic components." These "prophecies of doom" were made here Monday as leading scientists explored the question: Is there an optimum level of population?

The meeting was marked by predictions of famine, civil disorders and dictatorship in the 'third world' of developing countries. There were ominous warnings as to the reaction when people in those lands realize the extent to which they have been "plundered" of their mineral resources.[3]

The untrue and unproved presuppositions of these observations are almost monumental — that mineral resources are a fixed entity, unrelated to technology, that "dictatorship" is related to population, that human intelligence does not progress at a faster rate than human population. The popular origins of such pessimistic modes of thought are, of course, found in Malthus' famous essay:

> . . . the power of population is indefinitely greater than the power of the earth to produce and sustain man. Population, when unchecked, increases in geometrical ratio. Subsistence increases only in an arithmetical ratio . . . .
>
> Famine seems to be the last, the most dreadful resource of nature. The power of population is so superior to the power of earth to produce subsistence for man that premature death must in some shape or other visit the human race. The vices of mankind are active and able ministers of depopulation . . . .[4]

But if it is vice that ministers to depopulation, then virtue must minister to population so that modern followers of Malthus'

3. "Doom Forecast By Year 2000" (New York Times Press Service), *San Jose, California, Mercury,* 30 December 1969. Cf. also Walt Anderson, "Introduction," *Politics and Environment,* W. Anderson, editor, Pacific Palisades, Goodyear, 1970, pp. 1-9.

4. Thomas Robert Malthus, *Population: The First Essay,* Ann Arbor, Ann Arbor Paperbacks, 1960, pp. 3, 49.

psychology can reverse their definitions of virtue and vice in the light of this new "original sin" of increasing the population.[5]

However, this is not, scientifically, to establish the relation between starvation and population. It may well be that future starvation will be caused by too little rather than too much population if it turns out to be that it is human brainpower and genius, instead of a fixed earth, that determines what we can do and have. The United States seems to have been overpopulated at the time of the landing of Columbus.[6] The population of Europe today is considerably greater than that of the Roman Empire at its height. Yet, it would be rash indeed to argue that the Romans were better fed than today's French (especially French!), English, Italians, Spaniards, and Germans. There are, to be sure, some undernourished, even starving people today, however difficult it may be to define what exactly starvation may mean or to determine what is its exact cause.[7]

If we take as a norm the ideal minimum daily calorie, protein, and vitamin intake of today's health experts, for example, it is likely that most men who have ever lived were seriously undernourished in some sense. Furthermore, due to economics of scale and optimal growth rates, it is not altogether clear that the easiest way to improve human health and welfare on a large

5. For a recent adaptation of this thesis that virtue equals tragedy, cf. Rufus Miles, "Whose Baby Is the Population Problem?" *Population Bulletin,* 1 February 1970. It is interesting to note that Malthus was opposing the thesis of Mandeville in a way, for it was Mandeville's belief that progress was caused by our vices because vice creates demand. What Malthus and his followers have done is to substitute virtue for vice as the cause of change and then to make this change itself evil.

6. Cf. Colin Clark, "Do Population and Freedom Go Together?" *Fortune,* December 1960.

7. Cf. Michel Cépède, and others, *Population and Food,* New York, Sheed and Ward, 1964, Chapter 6, "How Food Production Has Developed," pp. 249-337; Ralph Thomlinson, *Population Dynamics,* New York, Random House, 1965, Chapter 14, "Population and Food," pp. 300-29; Colin Clark, *Population Growth and Land Use,* New York, St. Martin's Press, 1967, Chapter 4, "Population and Food," pp. 123-57.

scale is necessarily through a reduction in total human numbers or even through a drastic reduction of the birth rate to zero which so many critics seem to feel advisable if not absolutely necessary.[8]

Yet, the climate of concern about the population-food ratio is understandable enough. The total number of humans who have ever lived upon this planet has been variously calculated as anywhere from 77 to 83 billion people, of whom about four per cent are now alive.[9] On a linear time scale, the population of the earth at the beginning of the so-called first agricultural revolution some ten thousand years ago was about ten to twenty million. The population was one half billion about 1650; one billion was reached about 1850, two billion in 1930, three billion in 1960, and should reach four billion around 1975-80, and perhaps seven billion after the turn of the next century.[10] What has drawn most attention in these oft-cited figures is not just absolute numbers, which mean nothing in isolation from other figures, but increasing growth rates and ratios, with emphasis on doubling times of population. The basic questions remain: How dangerous are such rates in fact? Should they be controlled? How? To what are they to be compared? How is it possible to provide for human beings already alive at standards of health and well-being which themselves are constantly being upgraded?

8. For a discussion of population growth as a factor in economic development in the early modern period, cf. Phyllis Deane, *The First Industrial Revolution,* Cambridge, At the University Press, 1965, pp. 20-35, 254ff.

9. Cf. Garrett Hardin, *Population, Evolution, and Birth Control,* San Francisco, Freeman; Philip M. Hauser, "Recent Trends and Prospects," in *Population: The Vital Revolution,* Doubleday Anchor, 1964, p. 16; Philip M. Hauser, "World Population Growth," in *The Population Dilemma,* P. Hauser, editor, Englewood Cliffs, N. J., Spectrum, 1969, pp. 12-33.

10. Cf. John D. Durand, "A Long Range View of World Population Growth," *The Annals* of the American Academy of Political and Social Sciences, January 1967, pp. 1-8. Cf. also the various United Nations' *Demographic Yearbooks.*

That concern about population is now becoming almost commonplace in today's public media and political discussions is evident.[11] The "World Leaders' Declaration on Population," given to the United Nations in 1967, stated:

> Too rapid population growth seriously hampers efforts to raise living standards, to further education, to improve health and sanitation, to provide better housing and transportation, to forward cultural and recreational opportunities — and even in some countries to assure sufficient food. In short, the human life is being frustrated and jeopardized.[12]

President Richard M. Nixon's population policy statement in 1969 further seemed to associate population control with welfare.[13] Robert McNamara, in his current position at the World Bank, has tried to emphasize the drag increasing rates of population seem to place on development:

> As a development planner, I wish to deal only with the hard facts of population impact on economic growth. Recent studies show the crippling effect of a high rate of population increases on economic growth in any developing country. . . . In terms of the gap between rich countries and poor, these studies show that more than anything else, it is the population explosion which, by holding back the advancement of the poor, is blowing apart the rich and poor by widening the already dangerous gap between them.[14]

11. It is interesting, however, to note that concern about population has shifted from people to environment and nature in the United States in recent years.

12. "Statement on Population by World Leaders," Presented at the United Nations, 1967, New York, Population Council, 1968.

13. Cf. also President's Johnson's Committee's Report: "Population and Family Planning: The Transition from Concern to Action," Washington, Government Printing Office, 1968.

14. "Address of Robert S. McNamara to the Board of Governors of the World Bank," September 30, 1968, in *Population Bulletin,* November 1968, p. 74; Robert S. McNamara, "Address to the University of Notre Dame," 1 May 1969, Notre Dame, Indiana.

The ease with which development problems are tied to population trends, then, is a widely accepted factor in modern social thought.[15]

The problem of famine and population, however, presents a similar, curious division among the various authorities in the several scientific disciplines, a situation not unlike the division which we have noted earlier. Indeed, those secular sciences and disciplines that are more directly traced to Christian origins, such as economics and technology, become more and more the avowed enemies of the more radical population controllers.

> Both science and technology can clearly be seen to have their historical roots in natural theology and the Christian dogma of man's rightful mastery over nature. Therefore ... it is probably in vain that so many look to science and technology to solve our present ecological crisis. Much more basic changes are needed, perhaps of a type exemplified by the much-despised "hippie" movement, a movement that adopts most of its religious ideas from the non-Christian East. It is a movement wrapped up in Zen Buddhism physical love, and a disdain for material wealth. It is a small wonder that our society is horrified at hippies' behavior — it goes against our most cherished religious and ethical ideas ....[16]

Indeed, in this context, it should not go without notice that modern Asia and Africa are interested in precisely those elements in Western culture that cause development which are almost invariably of Christian origin. The consequences of this for the next century may be more profound than we are willing to acknowledge for it may be precisely these cultures which have to build

15. The best study of the intricate problems of development and population is probably that of Benjamin Higgins, *Economic Development,* W. W. Norton, 1968; cf. also the relevant chapters of G. Myrdal, *The Asian Drama,* The Twentieth Century Fund, 1968, 3 vols.

16. Paul Ehrlich, *The Population Bomb,* New York, Ballantine, 1968, p. 171. Cf. also for a much more thoughtful discussion of the relation between Eastern philosophies and recent movements, William Braden, *The Private Sea and the Search for God,* New York, Bantam, 1968.

for considerably larger populations that will bear the scientific
and technological elan which can provide for such a newer type
of advanced civilization.[17]

Economists, it seems, habitually write in a more hopeful
and positive manner about population, often counting it as a
necessary and vital element in economic growth.[18] Don Paarlberg's recent conclusion refuses the panic so typical of the more
radical population advocates:

> Our analysis thus carries us to this conclusion: that while
> direct food aid can be very helpful if wisely administered and
> kept at a moderate level, it is not a solution to the world
> food problem. If the food problem is to be met, it must
> be solved, with our help, primarily in the hungry nations
> themselves.
>
> This seems a possible thing. It may be that now, when
> the world is most alarmed about hunger, that ancient enemy
> is already in retreat. And the two events may be related. The
> alarm may have summoned the natural resources. The his-

17. Cf. Colin Clark, "World Power and Population," in *Politics and
Environment,* pp. 25-33.

18. Even economists who follow a general population control line
are much more cautious and optimistic than is common in population
discussions normally. Cf. for example, Ansley J. Coale, "Man and His
Environment," *Science,* 9 October 1970, pp. 132-36.

For general discussions of the relation of economics to population cf.
the following studies:

A. L. Levine, "Economic Science and Population Theory," *Population
Studies,* November 1965, pp. 139-54; A. H. Hansen, "Economic Progress
and Declining Population Growth," *American Economic Review,* March
1939; Richard A. Easterlin, "Effects of Population Growth on the Economic
Growth of Developing Countries," *The Annals,* January 1967, pp. 98-108;
Ansley J. Coale, "Population and Economic Development," *The Population
Dilemma,* Prentice-Hall/American Assembly, 1965, pp. 46-69; Carlo M.
Cipolla, *The Economic History of World Population,* Penguin, 1964;
William Peterson, *The Politics of Population,* Doubleday Anchor, 1964;
Barbara Ward, *Spaceship Earth,* New York, Columbia, 1965; Gavin W.
Jones, *The Economic Effect of Declining Fertility in Less Developed
Countries,* Population Council, 1969.

torian may write that ours was the generation that moved out from under the Malthusian shadow. Certainly, our generation is the first to see that this is possible . . . .[19]

From a technologist's viewpoint, Norton Ginsburg writes:

We should never forget that man has an enormous instinct for survival. When environmental conditions reach the point of extreme danger, I believe that men will adopt those measures which will guarantee the survival and even the improvement of the species. This may be an overly optimistic view, not shared by everyone. So I see the world, say, 2000, as an ecologically better balanced one than today's, full of enormous problems to be sure, but reflecting the incalculably great benefits of the new popular awareness that men have the power to create environment according to their images of what should be.[20]

19. D. Paarlberg, "Feed for More People and Better Nutrition," in *Overcoming World Hunger,* C. Hardin, editor, Prentice-Hall/American Assembly, 1969, p. 87.

Cf. also Clarence J. Engler, "Myths About the World's Food Supply," *Columbia,* August 1969, pp. 16-21; Lester Brown, "The New Agricultural Revolution," *Foreign Affairs,* July 1968; Robert T. Hall, "Interview, World Hunger," *US News,* 28 September 1970, pp. 66-69; Louis P. Reitz, "New Wheats and Social Progress," *Science,* 4 September 1970, pp. 952-55. "The Protein Gap," *WHO Chronicle,* February 1970, pp. 65-67; J. A. Schellenberger, "The Green Revolution Revisited," *Current,* September 1969, pp. 37-41.

20. Norton Ginsburg, "Question Marks About People-Environment Relationships," *Impact of Science on Society,* #2, 1970, p. 143.

"To my excitement I saw that the drift from sea and sky to the land of the more-with-less technology might inadvertently be amplifying the economic advantage of the 99% of humanity who live on the land in sufficient degree to promise doing so much more with what we have that we might prove Thomas Malthus and the economists wrong. This is and was possible because there was for the first time in history a dawning possibility through the more-with-lessing that we might be able to take care of all humanity at higher standards than any have ever known — this would in turn, if true, eliminate the war and the war technology which was predicated on the concept that there would never be

The more frank and realistic shadow of the economists and technologists serves again to emphasize how much world hunger is, in fact, a question of philosophy about the nature of the human being, about what he himself can do, and about what cannot be done to him. It is the conflicting scientific evidence itself that warrants our serious attention before we opt for a thoroughly pessimistic view of our future.

This can be seen more clearly by considering the thesis of the writers who *ex professo* believe that there is no real alternative to world starvation. What we are interested in here especially is both the facts and the theories that flow out of a selection of facts that seemingly support the thesis that there is no alternative to starvation. William and Paul Paddock, together with William Vogt and Paul Ehrlich, not to forget the perennial Julian Huxley, represent the extreme case in their analysis about how bad conditions really are.[21] It is of some interest, psychologically and intellectually, to see just how such writers arrive at their dire conclusions, what mental and cultural backgrounds they presuppose that incites them to arrive at such forebodings. For it is not just the facts that determine the philosophy, but the reverse, the philosophy determines the facts, which are to be

---

enough for more than a minority to survive and live out their potential life-span, wherefore war was intermittently recurrent.

I saw Malthus could be fundamentally wrong because his thoughts were devoid of any sense of technology's more-with-lessing." From *Utopia or Oblivion: The Prospects for Humanity* by R. Buckminster Fuller, p. 234. Copyright © 1969 by Buckminster Fuller, By permission of Bantam Books, Inc.

21. A more moderate statement of this mood would be that of George F. Kennan: "Not even the most casual reader of the public prints of recent months and years could be unaware of the growing chorus of warnings from qualified scientists as to what industrial man is now doing — by over-population, by plundering of the earth's resources, and by a precipitate mechanization of many of life's processes — to the intactness of the natural environment on which his survival depends." "To Prevent a World Wasteland," *Foreign Affairs*, April 1970, p. 401.

admitted, which are not. Perhaps more than in any other area, the relation between food and starvation is something that is conditioned by one's philosophy of man.

The first and most essential element in the approach of these writers who are willing to take almost any means to reduce population rapidly — both its rate and its absolute numbers — is a sense of panic that admits no way out.[22] The Paddocks propose a system of "tirage" based upon a concept of military medicine in which we allow to die those already lost in hope of saving survivors with the most likelihood of survival.[23] "But we need more interest and more influence from more people," William Vogt wrote in 1960 when population fever was just beginning to become widespread.

> We cannot afford the luxury of waiting for someone else to act. If we have any love for this earth and for the creatures that inhabit it, if we are concerned about our children's future, or even our own later years, it is we who must act.
>
> Not next week, nor tomorrow, Tonight! Today!
>
> If we have not passed the point of no return, it is coming closer at a terrifying speed. One resource for which there is no substitute is time.[24]

With the hindsight of some ten years, then, it is of some value to recall the major elements of someone like Vogt, who stands at the extreme end of the population theorists.

The essence of the thinking of Vogt and his more recent followers reveals a certain rigidity of economic and technological concepts. In a very real way, they are the "new conservatives" be-

22. Cf. the author's "The Urgency and the Waiting," *World Justice*, #4, 1969-70, pp. 435-59.

23. William and Paul Paddock, *Famine, 1975!* Boston, Little, Brown and Company, 1967, p. 205ff. (This chapter is reprinted in *Politics and Environment*, pp. 34-46.

24. William Vogt, *People!* New York, Sloane, 1960, pp. 18-19.

cause they have in one way or another given up any hope of the inventive and political genius of mankind finding an alternative other than the one they propose.[25] This is revealed especially in their emphasis on panic before problems that are described as being "insolvable." "Unless there is a marked change of course, we are drifting down a current that can only lead to Maelstrom." [26] And this is best perceived, supposedly, by hard headed realists who have — magical formula — actual experience:

> But men and women who have worked in this field (as opposed to verbalizing in the library or in the office), especially in backward countries, and who are not constrained by their official positions, will, I think, generally agree with me. Some, like Sir Charles Galton Darwin, will even be so pessimistic as to conclude that disaster is inescapable.[27]

In the light of this panic atmosphere — never noted to be a time for rational thought — the solutions of 1960, nevertheless, retained an ambiguity and simplicity that the more recent population controllers have frankly abandoned.[28]

Vogt, then, is capable of affirming that Japan has made the only "significant progress" in this question.[29] But later on in the same book, Vogt also implied that "frequent abortion . . . seems to be ethically unacceptable and physically damaging." [30] If this be the case, either Japan should not be praised or the ethics should be changed. Vogt still believed that massive foreign aid and

25. Again it is important to note the shift from concern about people which was the general climate of classical conservatism to concern about nature which is more similar to Rousseau and, philosophically, not really "conservative" at all by historical criteria.

26. Vogt, *op. cit.*, p. 208.

27. *Ibid.*

28. Compare, for example, the essays in *The Ecological Conscience*, Robert Disch, Englewood Cliffs, N.J., Spectrum, 1970, with *People!*

29. Vogt, *op. cit.*, p. 207.

30. *Ibid.*, p. 228.

development were necessary though he feared that this aid may have made matters worse.[31] In any case, we must, in Vogt's quaint and revealing phrase, cut down "the flow of babies as much as possible, at least for a few years." [32]

Who is preventing this desirable procedure of cutting down "the flow of babies?" Predictably, there is one major enemy which seems to bear the world wide responsibility — an influence which, to be sure, seems quite astonishing to most of its members. Indeed, it seemed astonishing to Vogt himself since the members of this powerful organization, the Roman Catholic Church, do not seem to adhere to its doctrines and reveal birth rates among themselves about on a par with others in their respective societies.[33] Be that as it may, "probably the major obstacle in doing this . . . is the Roman Catholic Church. This organization, more than any other, has denied birth control to the world's people." [34]

Since its members apparently do not practice what it preaches even in Vogt's terms, this corrupting influence must be sought through illicit lobbying and pressure on the American Government, the United Nations, and throughout other world political organizations.[35] As such, the Church is the primary enemy of world welfare, since that blissful concept is most easily reached, according to this school of thought, by population control. For Catholics, in their more cynical moments, it has to be rather amusing that what must be the greatest lobby of all time, the population lobby, considers the Church to be so effective as a power behind the scenes.

31. *Ibid.*, p. 210.
32. *Ibid.*, pp. 210-11.
33. *Ibid.*, p. 211ff. Cf. Judith Blake, "The Americanization of Catholic Reproductive Ideals," *Population Studies*, July 1966, pp. 27-43.
34. Vogt, *op. cit.*, p. 211. Ehrlich's book is, in many respects, little more than a diatribe on the Catholic Church.
35. Somehow, however, while it is "perverse" for there to be a "Catholic" lobby (if indeed there is one), it seems to be quite all right for the population groups to lobby all they want. This double standard is at least worthwhile noting once in a while just for the record.

Vogt, in common with so many in this field, is caught between a liberal attitude which formerly seemed to be required in American politics and the wrath he feels at the causes he believes to be at the root of world difficulties.

> If in this connection, (and I must affirm great respect and admiration for much of what the Church does), I write with some intolerance, it is because I have seen what this particular defender of "the natural law" has done to men, women, and children from New York to Latin America and Asia. Family overpopulation is probably the cause of more juvenile delinquency, poverty and general misery in the slums of New York, as well as other cities, than any other single factor.[36]

The structure of Vogt's argument is breathtakingly simple: this organization has prevented birth control means and information on a massive scale throughout the world. This resulted in overpopulation on a vast scale. But overpopulation is the essential cause of disease, hunger, and delinquency. So, therefore, the

36. Vogt, *op. cit.*, p. 211.

Julian Huxley's bitter comment is even more interesting: "We should support all legislation — state, national, international — that makes birth control easier and more socially approved. We must start discussion groups and civic action groups and bring pressure to bear on the United Nations and its agencies. For instance, on two occasions it has been proposed that the World Health Organization should take population density into consideration as a matter affecting the world's health. In both cases the proposal was rejected — so far as I can understand, entirely owing to pressure from Roman Catholic countries and organizations. This is an international scandal. If you can pretend that population pressure does not affect health, you can pretend anything." *The Human Crisis*, Seattle, University of Washington Press, 1963, p. 86.

Apparently, it is quite legitimate for Mr. Huxley to advocate pressuring state, national, and international organizations for his point of view, but a "scandal" when someone else does the same thing. And just how population affects health is one of the most difficult of all medical problems, cf. Jean-Michel van Gindertael, "Facing the 21st Century," *The UNESCO Courier*, March 1968; William Whyte, *The Last Landscape*, Doubleday Anchor, 1970.

Church is immoral and must be eliminated from the spheres of public policy so that this all-purpose remedy can be spread everywhere, to everyone.[37] This is a "medical" not a "theological" problem.[38]

Thus, having reduced the world population problem to such clear terms, apparently even in non-Catholic China and India, to Catholic opposition, Vogt, in 1960, was still, in spite of his pessimistic arguments, optimistic. "Given an unobstructed will, free of Roman Catholic opposition, with supporting funds amounting to a mere fraction of what is now being spent on space exploration, the possibilities are considerable." [39] It should not be difficult to teach women to use modern birth control means, especially as enlightened Asian governments want it.[40]

Vogt surveyed birth control means in 1960 — abortion, sterilization, condoms — and decided even these means would be sufficient without the development of the pill. It became a question of will, not means. Vogt cited the example of the Swedes before the Industrial Revolution who seemed to have reduced the birth rate without modern birth control technology. So apparently we may not even have to worry about the more recent developments. "Unless we are willing to concede superior intelligence on the part of the Swedes, there seems to be no reason why we should not expect comparable behavior from the Indians and some other people." [41]

This dated book of Vogt is, in retrospect, instructive when compared to the more recent and excited books of the same genre — notably those of Ehrlich and the Paddocks. For both of these later books, the situation is already too late. The curious methodology of *Famine, 1975* and *The Population Bomb* is to list all possible solutions to check famine or overpopulation,

37. Vogt, *op. cit.*, pp. 212-18.
38. *Ibid.*, p. 212ff.
39. *Ibid.*, p. 224.
40. *Ibid.*, p. 225.
41. *Ibid.*, p. 227.

then to conclude, reluctantly, that nothing will work.[42] "The collision is inevitable. The famines are inevitable," the Paddocks assure us.[43] Neither technology, nor ocean foods, nor population limitation, nor anything else will work. We can only salvage the few chosen. Paul Ehrlich goes so far as to advocate a reduction of the total world population to two billion.[44]

What is fascinating in these later books is the degree to which older liberal values of tolerance and respect for the beliefs of others are eroded. Karl Sax even tries to become a Christian and Communist theologian to explain to these bodies how they can accept population control within their own creeds.[45] Furthermore, — and this makes any opposition of the Catholic Church however strong or feeble seem useless anyhow — they have no patience with family planning or birth control as being really effective in the long run. In this, we can see just to what degree an approach such as that of Vogt is now out of date.

> The story in the underdeveloped countries is depressingly the same everywhere — people *want* large families. They *want* families of a size that will keep population growing . . . . It is important to remember that, even if women in the underdeveloped countries had exactly the number of children they wanted, the results would still be demographic catastrophe . . . . In fact, I know of no country in the world that has achieved true population control through family planning programs.[46]

42. Cf. also Karl Sax, *Standing Room Only,* Boston, Beacon, 1960.
43. Paddocks, p. 9.
44. Ehrlich, p. 79. "There are now too many human beings, and the problem is growing rapidly worse. It is potentially disastrous not only for the human race but for most other life forms as well. The goal would be half of the present world population, or less." Keith Murray, "Suggestions Toward an Ecological Platform," in *The Environmental Handbook,* p. 323.
45. Sax, pp. 176-91.
46. Ehrlich, pp. 83, 87. Cf. also Raid B. Tabbarach, "Birth Control and Population Policy," *Population Studies,* November 1964, pp. 187-96;

The final dashing of hope of family planning is, of course, what breaks down the liberal respect for human rights and opens the door to almost any birth control means — even those contrary to the admitted desires of the general population. This "elitist" element in population theorists is not something we can afford to ignore much longer.[47] It represents the collapse of any intellectual limit to what the state can do against the individual and the family in this area — Ehrlich's penalities against children are among the most frightful ever seen in modern literature — together with a complete pessimism with regard to the effectiveness of contemporary and future technological advances that demonstrates how far this style of thought is willing to go to achieve its dire ends.[48]

The authoritative British scientific journal, *Nature,* has warned of the dangers of scientific exaggeration coming from genetic and pollution sources, critics the journal calls "the Doomsday camp."[49] It clearly sees that we are confronted both with a question of fact — which does not support this Doomsday camp — and with a question of effort, since it is possible that this despair will shut off our studies and efforts to do something about the modern problems.

> The truth is that there have emerged in public opinion of science and technology a group of interlocking heresies . . . . The first and most obvious heresy is what may be called the pollution movement — an opinion that there is close at hand some kind of human catastrophe that will spring from the application of science in technology . . . . Certainly there is

Kingsley Davis, "Address," National Research Council Meeting, 14 March 1967.

47. Cf. Ben Wattenberg, "Overpopulation as a Crisis Issue: The Nonsense Explosion," *The New Republic,* 4, 11 April 1970, pp. 18-23.

48. Ehrlich, p. 136ff.

49. "On Which Side Are the Angels?" *Nature,* 27 December 1969, p. 1242.

no warrant for the strange prophesies which frequently suggest that disaster will spring from science and its application . . . . What is the truth? To begin with, there are sound technical reasons for believing that, in spite of what the Jeremiahs say, science and technology will contribute substantially to the solution of daunting problems. Is it not, after all, a simple fact that the world's food supply, measured in calories per head, has more than kept pace with the growth of population in the last thirty-five years, chiefly because of the improvement of agricultural productivity.[50]

This is a wise and healthy reaction from a solid scientific source since it sees clearly that the true danger that arises from the "hopeless" and "doomsday" — Gordon Rattray Taylor's latest book is even called *The Doomsday Book* — atmosphere of so many critics already cited is the danger of abandoning the efforts of man that can truly solve his problem. And, it should be clear, this is a moral choice, not scientific necessity.

It is, in one sense, more and more granted, even by the writers in population magazines, that the earth will really never come to a position in which it lacks adequate food. (We wonder if this is the reason why so many who follow this philosophy have shifted from fear of starvation to fear of pollution in recent years?)

In attempting to indicate what we know today about population and economic development, there is one important preliminary point. Many people have been alarmed by the population explosion and some writers have made forecasts of impending famine. However, although the population of the world today is larger than ever, the standard of living of a large proportion of mankind is also much higher than at any time in recorded human history. Equally, looking into the future, *it appears that the potential for economic growth is far greater*

50. *Nature*, pp. 1241-42.

than the potential for population growth. For instance, new strains of wheat, rice, and other foods have been discovered that could increase yields by two to five times over short periods of time. In contrast, the world population would only double over 35 years or so. Of course to exploit this potential would require large accompanying social changes, *but the potential is there, and it is immense.*[51]

This does not necessarily mean, as Mr. Zaidan goes on to suggest, that there is no argument for slowing down population growth rates. But it shows how much the nature of the population discussion must now begin to take real scientific and technical growth into account if it is to remain honest and reputable.

What is, however, much more interesting is the degree to which the theories of radical population control are based on a technology and economics that is considerably retarded and out of touch with what more visionary theories of human development propose. Again we suspect that the conservative models on which current population and pollution theories are built can only lead to scientific and human stagnation so that society will merely become a cyclic repetition of what went before, with no real impetus to change or grow. This is not, moreover, merely a question of wheat or rice tonnage, although even by contemporary agricultural standards themselves, it is very evident that food production based on presently programmed changes is rapidly progressing.[52] Again, it is not a question of advocating

51. George C. Zaidan, "Population Growth and Economic Development," *Studies in Family Planning*, May 1969, p. 1. Italics added.

52. Cf. Gerard Piel, "A World Free of Want?" *The Bulletin of the Atomic Scientists*, January 1968, pp. 16-22; Lester R. Brown, "New Directions in World Agriculture," *Studies in Family Planning*, June 1968, pp. 1-5; Theodore W. Schultz, "What Ails World Agriculture?" *The Bulletin of the Atomic Scientists*, January 1968, pp. 28-35; David Simpson, "The Dimensions of World Poverty," *Scientific American*, November 1968, pp. 27-35; Jurgen Heinrichs, *Hunger und Zukunft*, Gottingen, Verlag Vandenhoeck & Ruprecht, 1969; Tadd Fisher, "The Many-Faceted Food

maximum possible growth rates for population. Nevertheless, Professor Sauvy's caution is well to recall: "Not a single historical or present day instance can be cited of a declining or stagnating population that has enjoyed or is enjoying any real economic expansion." [53] There is, as Sauvy suggests, an optimum population size and an optimum growth rate. These are essentially political choices.[54] Nations can, as history shows, choose to decline.

Furthermore, not enough attention has been paid to the political and economic effects of low or zero population growth rates — at least not since Professor Hansen's suggestion that there was a relation between low birth rates and the depression.

The advantages of growth are still more striking in cases

Problem," *Population Bulletin,* December 1968, pp. 83-99; George A. W. Boehm, "Inexhaustible Riches from the Sea," *Fortune,* December 1963, p. 133ff.; Perry Stout, "Power: The Key to Food Sufficiency in India," *The Bulletin of the Atomic Scientists,* November 1968, pp. 26-28; *Overcoming World Hunger,* C. Hardin, editor, Prentice Hall/American Assembly, 1969; Norman Macrae, "The Neurotic Trillionaire," *The Economist,* 10 May 1969; Barbara Ward, *It Can Be Done,* London, Geoffrey Chapman, 1965; George Bylinsky, "Improving on Nature to Vanquish Hunger," *Fortune,* April 1969, p. 126ff.; Gabriel Bowe, *The Third Horseman,* Dayton, Pflaum, 1967; *The State of Food and Agriculture,* Rome, Food and Agricultural Organization, yearly; Richard J. Ward, "The Coming World Famine?" *America,* 14 September 1968; Conrad Taeuber, "Population and Food Supply," *The Annals,* January 1967, pp. 73-85; Colin Clark, *Population Growth and Land Use,* New York, St. Martin's Press, 1967, pp. 123-57; John McLaughlin, "The Ecology of Hunger," *America,* 11 September 1969; "Food Production — Shortage to Surplus," *Nature,* 3 January 1970, p. 9; Nevin S. Scrimshaw, "The Urgency of World Food Problems," in *Conditions of World Order,* S. Hoffman, editor, New York, Clarion, 1970; Gifford B. Pinchot, "Marine Farming," *Scientific American,* December 1970, pp. 15-21; J. George Harrar, *Strategy Toward the Conquest of Hunger,* New York, Rockefeller Foundation, 1967.

53. A. Sauvy, "Population Theories," in *International Encyclopedia of the Social Sciences,* New York, Macmillan, 1968, Vol. 12, p. 355.
54. *Ibid.,* p. 354ff. Cf. also J. J. Spengler, "Optimum Population Theory," *International Encyclopedia of the Social Sciences,* Vol. 12, p. 358ff.

where the proportions that need to be corrected are continually changing. This is especially true of technological progress and economic distribution of the labor force, not only among the three traditional sectors — primary, secondary, and tertiary — but also among the occupational subdivisions of each sector. In a stationary population with low mortality, the economically active population is replenished by the younger groups at a rate of only 2.2 per cent per year. Such a rate is not sufficient to ensure the occupational reallocation required by technological change. The result, relatively speaking, is an excess of people in obsolete trades and a consequent slowing down of economic progress.[55]

This analysis of Professor Sauvy is significant in that it takes into consideration the fact that technology itself and economic growth are themselves fostered by population growth. In a sense, no generation has adequate economic and technological imagination to understand how it is possible to solve future problems it does not itself have. The drive to reduce the contemporary popu-

---

55. *Ibid.*, p. 356. Professor Sauvy continues: "However, it is generally acknowledged that the spirit of enterprise does not flourish in an aging population; nineteenth-century France, and perhaps modern Ireland, are significant instances of this. Nor is an aging electorate the only factor. Not many new businesses are created when the generations hardly replace one another, since the younger generation is content to wait until jobs are vacated by the older. In such a population, most positions of power and responsibility are held by elderly people, and thus institutional rigidities set in . . . . The large proportion of one child families in a stationary population is another reason why the spirit of enterprise is weakened in both the older and younger families . . . .

Thus, the concept of optimum growth rate is better suited to an industrial economy. Generally, the more abundant or accessible natural resources are through international trade and the faster technological progress, the higher the rate of population growth should also be. For western Europe during recent years, a growth rate of between 0.5 and 1 per cent per year seems to have been necessary and by no means excessive."

lation rate to zero may well be the key to stagnation, not to growth or to a new concept of leisure or development.[56]

What is involved in this question is again a whole attitude toward man and nature, towards man's intelligence and his creativity. Professor Karl Brandt clearly emphasized the terms of the problem:

> There prevails a deplorable confusion even in basic economic and social concepts. One talks about resources as if they are a fixed given entity in a fixed geographical location. *To me the only genuine resources on earth, from which wealth can flow in ever increasing volume, are the intelligence, the skill, the creative mind, the determination to manage and work of the people.* I repeat — the only truly creative sources of wealth on earth are the human resources .... What is called "natural resources" is nothing but opportunities in the natural environment to apply man's genius to them to satisfy his changing needs and wants. What is a vital resource today may be a nuisance tomorrow — and vice versa.[57]

The type of society and economy we are entering today — entering because of human intelligence and skills — is not one that must follow previous forms of development and progress. There is a very definite sense in which food and well-being — even, in the future, nature itself — are the products of the human mind. Almost invariably, in spite of their attempt to consider themselves up-to-date, the great majority of predictions about

56. Cf. Clark, *Fortune*, December 1960.

57. Karl Brandt, "The Population Dilemma," *Vital Speeches*, 1963, pp. 629-30. Italics added.

"Why is the recognition of a creativity gap so important for developing countries? In the long run, it is probably not so much the acquiring of scientific and technological expertise that alone determines the long-range direction and quality of a country's industrial and technological progress, but the quality of its creative and innovative impulse." Bernard T. S. Tan, "The Creativity Gap and Developing Countries," *The New Scientist*, 14 May 1970, p. 330.

world famine and ecological disaster are based upon technical and scientific and economic concepts that are already surpassed. The reasons why this is not more obvious than it is, it seems to be evident, are primarily philosophical ones, having to do with an outlook and an attitude toward man and his place in the universe.

This is not to say that starvation is non-existent nor that it absolutely cannot happen on a major scale. But rather that if it does happen, as we suggested earlier, the reason will lie in the human will, not in a deficiency of nature or human intelligence. Indeed, one sometimes wonders whether too many groups and population philosophers do not have a kind of vested interest in the failure of man to provide for his increasing numbers on a more adequate scale. One can legitimately wonder today in the changed climate of opinion, whether had this climate existed ten years ago, the philanthropic and governmental organizations recently responsible for increased food yields throughout the world would have initially begun their research that resulted in such great improvements. Had they not, would it really have proved the thesis of the population "explosionists," as Ben Wattenberg calls them? The advanced and radical optimism of a Buckminster Fuller cannot be admitted because it fundamentally undermines the inadequate foundations on which the famines and the poverty and the doomsday are confidently predicted.[58] The trouble with

58. "The prime design must also provide for the orderly transfer of the world consumer population from the obsoleting worker payrolls to the world educational system's advanced search, research and vital regeneration functioning. Einstein's norm of constantly transforming evolutionary patterning must designedly replace Newton's now invalidated static order.

Prime designing augments wealth. Wealth permits increased freedom of personal time investment. Prime design may multiply the alternate physical facilities for desirable anatomical, mental, and cultural development. Desirable time investment alternatives inherently decrease over-all "baby-making" time. That explains "the rich getting richer and the poor getting children." Prime designing commands the fundamental solution of the over-population threat. As with all fundamental problems of man

so many current population theories, then, is that they are based on social and economic concepts that could do nothing but retard and hinder the human in its physical and moral growth.[59]

The physical requirements of man in this life — food, shelter, clothing, education — have been dependent upon engineering and agricultural concepts that are themselves intrinsically limited. Too much of the population scare is based upon the thesis that these intrinsic limitations — based on concepts of the recent past and therefore "conservative" in that sense, usually anti-urban in bias — cannot be overcome within the concepts governing any future discussion. It may be correct — but even this is somewhat doubtful — that *current* concepts cannot do the long-range job. We must note, for example, that more recent literature is beginning to be more worried about surpluses than scarcity and that our international organizations have themselves been somewhat biased in their presentation of the facts:

> The latest annual report of the Food and Agricultural Organization of the United Nations is a more realistic document than many previous numbers of the series. Sensibly enough, the report openly acknowledges that there has been a sustained increase of food production in the past few years. . . . In the past, the temptation to urge on readers

on earth, fundamental solutions are not to be had by political reforms of either the peacetime prohibitory law enforcement variety, or of the never convincing wartime annihilation variety. Fundamental solutions are not for sale. Mass subscriptions to support professional do-gooders are futile.

Fortunately population explosion is only the momentary social hysteria's cocktail conversation game. Real population crisis is fundamentally remote." R. Buckminster Fuller, "Prime Design," *Ideas and Integrities,* New York, Collier, 1963, p. 248. Cf. Fuller, *Utopia or Oblivion,* Chapters 10 and 11.

59. The current trend to oppose nature to technology, furthermore, and then to attack population in its name is both anti-city in its origins and oblivious to the degree to which nature is also dependent on man.

the danger of still growing population of the Earth has often been too strong for the authors of these reports. Now, however, it does seem clear that when seasonal ups and downs are ironed out, food production is increasing if anything more quickly than the population. For the world as a whole, for example, food production per head is now about 10 per cent greater than in the early fifties and, as the annual report of the FAO makes plain, the improvement in the Far East has been particularly marked — a total increase of 14 per cent in these years.

But what of the more distant future? The most obvious danger is that there may in due course be such a large increase of population that no amount of increased efficiency in agriculture will be able to provide for it. This, however, is still very much an academic matter. For one thing, the way in which the graphs of population and food production have kept more or less in step for the past thirty years suggests that demand can effectively stimulate supply without bumping up against physical limitations of an absolute character. Second, the population statistics on which these calculations are inevitably based take very little account of the way in which the birth rate has been declining in several countries in the past few years.[60]

60. "Food for the Crowds," *Nature,* 12 December 1970, p. 1015. Cf. also "Food for the Future," *Nature,* 12 December 1970, p. 1021.

"It is, of course, high time that the Food and Agricultural Organization acknowledge the steady progress there has been in agricultural productivity. Only three years ago, Mr. B. R. Sen, the then Director General of FAO, set out to chill the marrows of those not dying of starvation with tales of how disaster might be round the corner. Although this message was even then an obvious exaggeration (*Nature,* 212, 330, 1966), the past three years have shown clearly enough that *there is no technical problem in making sure that food production grows faster than the population.* The new strains of wheat, maize and rice which are being introduced to farmers in the Middle and Far East are only the most dramatic and recent sign of what may be accomplished and, indeed, their influence has

Yet, even the successes of recent efforts which are now being felt do not take into consideration the manner in which design engineers, technologists, chemists, and economists have been thinking about the very nature of food itself, of clothing, of shelter, of all the realities of physical life. There is an even more vast and radical abundance on our doorstep whose potential almost requires for its reality a population on a scale much more vast than anything that we yet know. Further, we are beginning to learn that the sources and types of energy available to us are for all practical purposes unlimited.[61] This suggests that all thought based on the finiteness of our fossil fuels or even on our agricultural land areas is coming to be irrelevant.

The crucial aspect is to understand the degree to which items of scarcity and nature are more and more replaceable so that the human intelligence can begin to think of an infinity of power and production, an almost complete interchangeability of natural and synthetic materials so that what is needed is produced from what is most abundant, not from what is scarce. John McHale, whose book *The Future of the Future* is essential for any discussion of population and the nature of future society, has vividly presented this newer spirit that has challenged and changed the older economic and technological concepts on which most thinking about population has been based.

In our most recent development we have begun to learn how to learn, how to invent and even to institutionalize, or create, favorable climates for the encouragement of creativity

---

only barely begun to make a mark on statistics . . . . What this implies is that the FAO and its parishioners can realistically look forward to a steady expansion of agricultural industry and to an avoidance of the old Malthusian catastrophe." "Malthus Can Turn in His Grave," *Nature,* 3 January 1970, p. 1.

61. Cf. Max Born, "Reflections of a European Man of Science," in *On Modern Physics,* W. Heisenberg and others, New York, Clarkson N. Potter, 1961, pp. 57-78; A. R. Ubbelohde, *Man and Energy,* Pelican, 1963; S. Handel, *The Electronic Revolution,* Pelican, 1967.

and innovation. Clearly our way forward lies with the more conscious and reflective control of much that has been unconsciously carried forward.

The way beyond the exponentials lies between evasive optimism and an equally dangerous, but more inhibiting despair. It requires, rather, a cool pragmatism that affirms a strong belief in man's innate capacity to solve his problems, but covers its bets by more consciously devising and applying the ways and means to avoid catastrophe.

Our chances for survival are closely based on a capacity to meet the largest challenge ever offered to man. Technologies and "know-how" are more than adequate to solve many of our largest problems. What we lack is that combination of vision, industry and innovative action that will enable us to use our knowledge more inmmediately and more effectively.[62]

It is evident why this kind of a scientific-humanist approach to our problems of population and poverty radically supercedes the attitudes that have pervaded the organizations professionally devoted to population control. It explains too why these organizations, in their more aware moments, are beginning to be evading the food issue and shifting to such intangible concepts as "stress" and "natural" environment conceived in quite romantic terms to explain the continuing pressure they wish to see us under.

McHale has suggested that the essential weakness in the thesis of so many population analyses lies in their use of mathematical projections and their failure to take into account the vast changes in the scientific and technical communities. In fact, the work of such men as Fuller, McHale, Calder, and others has so drastically changed the intellectual context of population studies that we

62. John McHale, *The Future of the Future*, New York: George Braziller, Inc., 1969, p. 170. It is important to note that J. J. Revel, in his *Ni Marx Ni Jésus* (Paris, Lafont, 1970), has based his whole theory of the importance of the United States in the contemporary world on this kind of inventive capacity.

may well wonder whether most thinking on this subject is not now simply obsolete — except to the degree that its very success in controlling population may prevent these newer possibilities from ever coming to be. As McHale suggests, the whole earth has now become available to man in a way it never was before, indeed, knowledge is coming rapidly to enable us to use the very building blocks of the universe in any way we choose. What is really happening is more likely a jump in the population to take advantages of the newer forms of human life required for this more developed form of life.[63] The significance of this is that it begins

63. "But we must discount much of the more simplistic extrapolation of exponentials that has been adduced so far. Exponential curves do not grow in isolation; they are related to other growths and values, in simplest relation: as one value goes up, its opposite goes down. As Price says: "In the real world things do not grow and grow until they reach infinity. Rather, exponential growth eventually reaches some limit, at which the process must slacken and stop before reaching absurdity. The more realistic function is also well known as the logistic (or S) curve, and it exists in several slightly different mathematical forms.

Growth, size, and change itself are all relative measures. What looks like separate rates of increase of abnormally explosive growth is one narrow frame of reference, such as a span of time, may be a slowly changing distribution relative to a wider context or longer time span.

Human beings are not fruit flies, and while their aggregate activities may conform to the natural growth patterns, the point of plateauing in human trends is not necessarily saturation before the onset of decay, but may be a more or less consciously exercised control function.

The numbers game itself is not infallible — even though its more skilled and scientific operators bid fair to become our new theocracy! Adequate statistical compilations are of recent origin, and in many areas are still crudely approximate. Their enthusiastic and over credulous use in recent years is often more reflective of the human need for some stable authority image ("figures can't lie") than it is for the reliability and predictive accuracy that statistics claims . . . .

The growth of population may have been retarded for centuries, and may now be climbing swiftly toward a new optimal size required by the next phase of human development. Decreasing amounts of land per capita, though often cited as an obvious limiting factor of human expansion, is a relative measure and is crucial only during a critical transition period . . . . As we have noted man has now expanded his ecological niche to include the whole planet. His activities are no

to enable us to escape from the narrow confines of traditional concepts of economic and historic models on which population discussions have been based.

Expansion of the environmental capacities of man to include all the earth's air, water, and land surface, in addition to the constant recycling of material goods themselves, is now within reach. This is again a function of the growth of intelligence itself, the development in practice of the theology and philosophy that affirm that the earth is for man and to be used by him — indeed, of the belief that the natural earth itself is not complete in its own perfection as earth without the addition that comes from the addition of human intelligence to it. The economics of abundance is only the beginning of newer concepts in which the mass availability of energy and information, the automatization of labor itself makes available to the human race an adequacy and superfluity of hitherto scarce items so that they appear as normal and almost free natural items like air.[64] The growth rate of practically all things human approach infinity when considered by themselves. "Then (1940), the rate of development shot upwards exponentially," Professor Milton Harris wrote recently. "During the ensuing 25 years the gross national product grew seven-fold from $100 billion to $700 billion and R & D budgets nearly ten times faster from $400 million to more than $25 billion. The speed of travel increased fifty-fold; our ability to handle data grew by a factor of 1 million; our energy resources increased a

___

longer constrained to horizontal deployments around its surface, but go increasingly into and beyond the atmosphere, beneath the earth, and deep into the oceans." McHale, pp. 160-63.

64. The real danger we do face is the widespread disdain that is now beginning to infect the social community for pure research and continued advanced education. Cf. Philip Handler, President of the US National Academy of Science, "Somber Greetings from Abroad," *Nature*, 27 December 1969, p. 1250. The address of Professor Handler's predecessor is also significant in this regard: Frederick Seitz, "Science, the Universities and Society," *The American Scientist*, Autumn 1968, p. 295ff.

thousand-fold." [65] The growth rates of practically all things human approach infinity when considered in themselves. What has happened is that the confluence of all of these rates, together with population, make the fuller human life all politics and economics from the beginning of time have hoped for now to be possible, even necessary.[66]

In the area of food production itself, there is a recent upturning in estimates about the success of recent agriculture. The European Common Market, for instance, has experienced a record production of cereals:

> The EEC's wheat surplus in 1969 was around 4 million tons about 12 per cent of normal production — and its accumulated surpluses (on the gloomiest estimate of what exactly is "surplus") at the end of that harvest about 12 million tons of which about 3 million tons will be used internally as fodder. For comparison every year the United States and Australia have to find export markets for about 40 to 50 per cent of their output, and Canada more.
>
> There is no clear line between surplus production and production for export. The largest single reason why the EEC's silos are bursting is that everyone else's are too: the world wheat market is simply glutted.[67]

The same sharp increases in agricultural potential is noted in other parts of the world also.[68]

65. Milton Harris, "The Paradoxical Years," Perkins Medal Award Address, *Chemical and Engineering News,* 2 March 1970, p. 54.

66. Cf. Robert Theobald, *The Challenge of Abundance,* Mentor, 1961; Robert Theobald, *An Alternative Future for America,* Chicago, Swollow, 1970, Martin Bronfenbrenner, "The Economic Consequences of Technological Change," *Values and the Future,* ed. K. Baier and N. Rescher, New York, The Free Press, 1969, pp. 453-71.

67. "EEC Farm Policy," *The Economist,* 28 March — 3 April 1970, p. 35.

68. Cf. footnote #52.

But there is another even further consideration. No one today objects to wearing nylons, dacrons, and other synthetic fibres. Will agriculture itself become technologically unnecessary, at least in great part. With the present phase of the scientific revolution, it is not only necessary to look at improvements in nature such as new wheat or rice, but also to the complete by-passing of many intermediate states of development to go into direct food productions either from vegetable or inert matter. Archibald McPherson's essay, "Synthetic Food for Tomorrow's Billions," is significant because it recalls graphically how we cannot, in our necessary pursuit for new solutions, be strictly ruled by past social organizations or modes of production. Nigel Calder has similarly argued, adding the fact that by this process we could return a good part of our agricultural land to forests and grasslands.[69]

"The ultimate solution to the problem," McPherson writes, "must lie in a totally new source of food that will relieve the world's population from virtually sole dependence on agriculture." [70] The advantages of working in this direction are enormous since they avoid in part the sociological and political difficulties inherent in transforming world agriculture along more traditional lines.

Conventional methods of increasing food production, for example through agriculture and fisheries, cannot be expanded rapidly enough to provide this critical increase. Too many people are involved, and in many places the profound social changes required cannot be brought about quickly. We must turn from agriculture to the production of food by syn-

69. Nigel Calder, *Eden Was No Garden*, New York, Holt, Rinehart, and Winston, 1967.

70. Archibald T. McPherson, "Synthetic Food for Tomorrow's Billions," *Beyond Left and Right*, R. Kostelanetz, editor, New York, Morrow, 1968, p. 212. The book of Calder is an extensive presentation of this whole position.

thesis. Synthesis of large quantities of food that are basically identical with natural food can be achieved by relatively small numbers of people using readily available raw materials in facilities that can be set up and duplicated almost anywhere in the world.[71]

McPherson is not proposing a catch-all, nor is he advocating any less stress on modernizing conventional agriculture which itself is so rapidly changing. Rather he is again insisting that we recognize the broader type of thinking and research that is already available and necessary to confront the food problems of the human race.

Buckminster Fuller's essay on modern housing is also an analogous instance of the unconventional thinking necessary to convince us that we can improve and increase our radical capacities to cover the globe in ever-increasing qualitative improvement if we are willing to expand our horizons enough to see the limitations of our present population size and the technology on which it is based.[72] Fuller suggests that it is only by going out of conventional concepts and systems, by seeing that vast potential that is laid up in human enterprise and intelligence, the incredible potentiality of nature itself, that the seemingly enormous problems of one generation or mode of thought become normal and comparatively easy to a further stage of growth.

The apparent dilemma of food and population, then, is not really a problem of uncontrolled birth rates. Birth rates are important, to be sure, and both falling and rising birth rates may cause serious problems. But there are extremes on both sides. The reduction of all modern problems to the issue of population control, however, is both an intellectual escapism and a lack of faith due to man's capacities. Indeed, it is curious the degree to which this should be so. What we require is a much vaster and

71. *Ibid.*, pp. 216-17.
72. Cf. Buckminster, "Preview of Building," *Ideas and Integrities*, pp. 269-70. Cf. also pp. 146-72; 199-224.

more solid base on which we can both protect the humanity of man and provide for his potentials. His capacities are so much greater than we have been willing to admit that we are at this moment in something of a crisis of self-confidence that could well retard mankind for the next thousand years. McHale's observation is apt:

> The conceptual extension is towards a planetary ecology which assumes that its prior concern is with the maintenance of the planetary society. In using this approach, however, we tend to go beyond the "systems" approach of the natural and social ecologists. We deemphasize the control of natural laws and the closed determinism of a more rigorous systems analysis of the forces operable in ecological processes, and we concentrate instead on human communication and response . . . .

> Our approach here is only a conceptual recognition that the *natural world is not solely modified by physical forces; beyond a certain period in human development on earth, this modification also emanates increasingly from human acts within the environment.* It recognizes also that such acts are not confined to physical exploitation and transformations of the earth to achieve various economic purposes, but include those that are less amenable to direct perception and measure and which comprise our social and cultural symbolic systems.

> Our individual and collective actions have now moved to a scale and degree of possible negative or positive adaptability, which suggests that we must also move, concomitantly, to assume conscious responsibility for the overall stewardship of this planet.[73]

It is this priority of the human and its grasp of its relation to planetary nature that constitutes the solidity of this approach to nature and ecology.

73. McHale, pp. 65-65. Italics added.

We are being given increased alternatives — we can tamper with the very structure of man as the geneticists propose, we can despair with the population controllers who wish to limit the human race to a level of two or three billion at technological levels well below what man is capable of, since the technological and scientific and human potential in man is itself proportioned to the number of people that are in the world. We can, on the other hand, really grasp what is potential to us, both what we are from nature and what we can do with our planet. We can, if we wish, create a quality of life far beyond that which we know. And yet, we have our past. It is part of us, as valuable to us as our future. We have too our natural world which we wish to beautify and evolve more into our very lives. The human, the natural, the past, the future, the mind, the body — these are not contradictory things which we cannot live with. Yet, we cannot live with them all together unless we believe we can. The confusion of food and population is, ultimately, a spiritual problem.

REVOLUTIONARY THREATS TO HUMAN EQUALITY
AND VALUE

5 Modernity in the realm of social theory begins with the notion that the future form and quality of human life is now the result of choice and deliberate selection rather than natural evolution. And this is true even should man choose to remain essentially what he has historically been. Indeed, this is the crux of the contemporary problem about man. Is his "structure" more than an arbitrary result of statistically interacting forces with no further plan beyond their own visible result so that all conceivable rational, evolutionary, and contrived forms of man would be metaphysically identical and equal? In spite of the best efforts of modern philosophy, we are not yet done with cosmic teleology since it is only if man is, in some sense, more than a minor mathematical and planetary accident that we need worry about "saving" him.

But it is not merely the scientific restructure of man that presents itself as normative as a guide for what man should do with the earth and with himself. The conservation-ecological schools of recent years have taken as their model of man not the form into which he might be refashioned, but natural man before he evolved his scientific and cultural capacities.

> Personal revulsion aside, the lesson of this environmental assault by the oil companies (in Alaska) . . . is that an ecological conscience has far from permeated our civilization.
>
> The public conscience, however, has at last become uneasy. And there are enough of us to insist that a truly representative sample of all the earth's unique and as yet only moderately manhandled environment be completely withdrawn from exploitation. . . .
>
> It is, in short, a last Arctic frontier that must be given the legal protection of the Wilderness Act. Protected not only to save its unique biota but to provide a last retreat where men may test themselves so that they will not lose all those qualities of wind, muscle, and uprightness bred into our species during 99% of the last million years when we were hunters and food-gatherers.[1]

1. "Aububon View," *Aububon*, September 1970, p. 132.
"The following thesis may provide some useful insights into these problems: we are in an environmental crisis which threatens the survival of this nation, and of the world as a suitable place of human habitation. Environmental pollution is not to be regarded as an unfortunate but incidental by-product of the growth of population, the intensification of production, or of technological progress. It is rather, an intrinsic feature of the very technology which we have developed to enhance productivity. Our technology is enormously successful in producing material goods, but too often is disastrously incompatible with natural environmental systems. Yet, the survival of all living things — including man — the quality of life, and the continued success of all human activities — including technology, industry, and agriculture — depends on the integrity of the complex web of biological processes which comprise the environment — the earth's ecosystem. And what man is now doing on the earth violates this fundamental requisite of human existence. With tragic perversity

As we have suggested earlier, this approach also begins to devise means to refashion man because his presence in the world has no theoretic specialness about it which enables him to guide it for his own purposes. Therefore, here, too, it becomes necessary to institute those perversions and deviations into human life which can control population in the name of nature.

But the choice to remain human is itself more than a little ambiguous since the enlargement of freedom — which seemingly results from an expansion of the number of actual physical possibilities open to the being of man — is not necessarily identical with the expansion of human dignity itself. This does not mean, to be sure, that the fact that man must now choose to remain what he is does not represent an advance in the dignity that man has been given. The great value of man is, in a very real sense, that he has the ultimate choice of affirming what he is in the radical physical sense of accepting his historical being. But this also suggests that the possibility of rejecting historical man is also a real threat.

For a good segment of modern humanist theory, indeed, the formation of the new man consists precisely in the conscious rejection of the basic elements of man as he has been received from nature. Many trends in population theory, genetics, ecology, biology, and medicine, it has been suggested, have demonstrated how fundamental this rejection can potentially be. In other words, the selection of change must still answer the question of deformity. That is, is the "new" man that can be caused to be really something superior to man as we have known him? Or is the "natural" man that we want to preserve as something of the environment really a norm that would serve human betterment? The deliberate choice of monstrosity or deformity is itself faustian. We are never free

we have united much of our production economy to precisely those features of technology which violate the environment that supports it." Barry Commoner, "Soil and Fresh Water: Damaged Global Fabrid," *Environment,* April 1970, p. 5.

to praise change or preservation merely because it is possible. Possibility remains ever subject to intelligence and purpose.

The implications of the various views about the structure and restructure of man are not always clearly enough spelled out. We have already noted that a growing group of ecological thinkers take as a model man and earth as it has evolved to the present — or better, man and earth before the advent of population and technology. This essentially conservative model then becomes a weapon to attack scientific theories which hold that man to develop can and should totally transform the earth and its environs. The revolutionary version of this position is to attack "developed" countries on the ground, itself scientifically relative and out-of-date, that these countries are consuming more than their "share," — as if "share" were somehow a stable, definite, measurable thing, unrelated to scientific development.[2]

Here, however, we are more concerned with the concrete theories and proposals of the geneticists and social theorists about the nature and need for a revolutionary change in man as we have known him. What is of interest, then, is especially that aspect of this discussion that refers to sex, family, and population, itself the natural consequences of sex and family. For it is most radically that aspect of the "human" which originates in the very distinction of the sexes that is beginning to be most fundamentally questioned by contemporary radical and genetic theory. In one sense, as we have already seen, heterosexuality, as the normal and optimal way to guarantee the propagation and protection of the race, is called into question because it is, conceivably, no longer required to guarantee the future of the species.[3]

2. The very notion of resources, raw materials, goods is related to knowledge and energy potentials which vary incredibly from generation. Furthermore, there is a sense in which energy and resources are not lost but change form so that there is a certain reversibility in nature that is related to knowledge and energy.

3. Cf. R. P. Michael, "Bisexuality and Ethics," in *Biology and Ethics,* F. J. Ebling, editor, London, Academic Press, 1969, pp. 67-72.

Why this suggestion needs further analysis, then, is because it is offered as a natural and logical consequence of human progress. Indeed, it is offered as a cure for society's ills. Though he is not directly treating this topic, Professor Morton Kaplan has suggested some of the crucial problems that we may be faced with. Kaplan is attempting to elaborate a defense of systems analysis in which he is concerned to establish the system itself and not its origin as the more scientific, even the more ethical basis upon which to judge results.

> . . . If the biological revolution permitted us to synthesize the ovum and sperm cell, to fertilize the egg, and to grow the fertilized egg in an artificial culture, we could produce an equivalent human being. This may or may not be beyond the ingenuity of man, but in principle it illustrates the point. The appropriate distinction is not between the unconscious designs of nature and accident on the one hand and the conscious and purposeful designs of men on the other but between the kinds of systems to which the generalizations are applied . . . . If the likeness of the artificially created human to natural humans were overlooked, the moral consequences would be monstrous.[4]

Kaplan's hypothetical conclusion is undoubtedly correct, granted its effectuation, but the real question remains: what happens to humanity itself in this concept when the very being of man is under an artificial process? Clearly his structure is then irrelevant except as the historical source from which men learned how to replace it. Or is the human imitation of natural beings according to which new beings are the results of human rather than natural intervention a reason to give the artificial beings a status different from the natural ones?

4. Morton A. Kaplan, "Traditionalism vs. Science in International Relations," *New Approaches to International Relations*, M. Kaplan, editor, New York, St. Martin's Press, 1968, pp. 5-6.

The metaphysical overtones of the questioning of the place of sex cannot be ignored, for they imply that it is precisely in the overcoming of the 'natural" sexual function that the new man is to be produced (or in the case of the nature-ecologists, pre-served). For the being "male" and the being "female" — which are called "accidents" even in classical thought — introduce into the very midst of being itself a profound variation.[5] The radical relation of the male and the female is profoundly diverse. They do not perform the same function. What they are is defined by their potential relation to their sexual functions and their paternal or maternal roles. But is this variety of function, this "inequality" if it is proper to speak in this manner, is it essentially "unjust," is it the kind of inequality that represents a metaphysical violation of being itself so that its consequences must be rescinded?

If the origins of natural inequalities such as those represented in the heterosexual distinction are in no sense "normative," that is, without teleological origins, then, of course, the denial of the inequality or diversity of the sexes — either in function or in physical fact — becomes exactly the program according to which the "new" man is to be formed. All of these "traditions" of family and society based upon the natural distinction of the sexes will have to be seen as somehow "abnormal" or at least as neutral *vis-a-vis* what man supposedly can do.

In classical Aristotelian thought, the natural world was con-sidered to be fundamentally teleological, that is, there was a pur-pose in the cosmic order and a hierarchy of beings. This meant ultimately that there was a "higher" and a "lower," a "good" and a "bad," but the existence of a higher and a lower, a good and a bad was necessarily connected with the broader ontological problem of a common good in which diversity and evil received their resolution in some more profound order which elevated the

5. Cf. Aristotle, *Ethics,* Book VII; *Politics,* Books I, II; cf. Gertrude von le Fort, *The Eternal Woman,* M. Buehrie, trans., Milwaukee, Bruce, 1954.

existence of inequality, difference, and evil into a meaningful and necessary part of finite possibility. The alternative to inequality, diversity, and evil is precisely *nothing,* non-existence, so that the profound affirmation of being, of actual possibility is the simultaneous recognition of the purposiveness of the reality that is.[6]

Man, in this system, stood at the apex of the physical order because he could himself "understand." But understanding meant discerning a natural order so that the differences and inequalities observed in man and nature were preserved and ordered to a good of the whole. In this sense, man as he naturally and historically evolved was not merely accidental. The existence of natural differences or inequalities was the premise upon which the human condition itself existed. The very concepts of drama, art, and the state depended upon these distinctions. Indeed, it seems, both the state and the family depend for their intrinsic worth upon the fundamental value and normalcy of the heterosexual distinction. It is not without interest that classical literature and the state rise or fall with the continued and varied relation of the sexes to one another. Part of the so-called "revolution" in modern literature is, at bottom, connected with this questioning of the normalcy of the distinction between the sexes and its social implications.[7]

The basic political concepts of equality, constitutional, and political rule were taken in classical thought from the model of the family which was understood to be based upon the most obvious and radical distinction within the human, that is, between the sexes. This inequality or diversity of function symbolized most graphically by the fact that only females bear children was considered to be of deliberate design. When Aristotle spoke of this natural distinction in the *Politics,* he pointed out that "there must

6. Cf. Frederick Sontag, *God, Why Did You Do That?* Philadelphia, Westminster Press, 1970.

7. Cf. Joseph Wood Krutch, "Must Writers Hate the Universe?" *Saturday Review,* 6 May 1967, pp. 19-21.

be a union of those who cannot exist without each other; namely, of male and female, that the race may continue...." (1252a28-30). The context of natural reproduction, then, is that of immortality, the attempt to overcome the natural finiteness of man.[8] Man does not conclude to the necessity as a result of his own choice, but finds himself within its very ambitus by virtue of the fact that he is already created male and female. The result of this distinction and purpose is, in the sexes, that there is "a natural ruler and subject, that both may be preserved" (1252a31). Aristotle saw the sexual diversity as a means of preserving the human itself by preserving the sexes. The male and the female are distinctions that themselves preserve a greater good.

The woman is different from the slave because the woman retains her unique distinction as female. The barbarians, according to Aristotle, did not distinguish between the differing functions of male and female. The result was that "there is no natural ruler among them" (1252b6). Consequently there is an indiscriminate mixture of male and female among them which results ultimately in the destroying of the sexual distinction itself.[9]

In the household, there are two relations of natural freedom, that of father-son, that of husband-wife (1259a40). The "inequality" of male and female is, normally, permanent (1259b 10). But their relationship is "constitutional," that is, there is full freedom in the woman so that her function is rational and free within the family and in regard to the man. She is to understand, as it were, how the very fact of her distinction itself contributes to the very notion of sexuality and the family, hence to her own happiness and that of mankind. It is in the state, however, where the models of equality — the analogate is the relation

8. Cf. Hannah Arendt, *The Human Condition,* The University of Chicago Press, 1958.

9. For Aristotle, this distinction was itself necessary for the good both of the race and of the individual.

of brothers to one another — and of rule — the analogate is the relation of father to his own son — and of constitution — the analogate is the relation of husband and wife — come to perfection among citizens. Without these natural distinctions and the virtues based upon them, the concepts of authority and equality become unintelligible, that is, they disappear since there is no reason for them.[10]

There is a basic and obvious sense, then, in which the diversity of the sexes, their basically different experience as it relates to their own separateness and to the child, makes it a good that they are unequal, that is, that the male and the female have divergent, in a sense, incomparable experiences. Professor Norman O. Brown has introduced the phrase "polymorphous perversity" into our vocabulary.[11] This is a significant concept in the evolution of the present discussion. "Political and fleshly emancipation," Brown writes, "are finally one and the same; the god of Dionysus." [12] This is an effort to argue that the natural distinction upon which politics — and more radically metaphysics — was philosophically built in classical thought is to be overcome by a new kind of concrete, non-abstract human interchange that is "polymorphous" and "perverse" with respect to traditional normalcies which found virtue and strength only in the basic male-female relationship.

In Aristotle's sense, there could be no "natural" rule nor any "constitutional" relationship between male and female in this new concept, that is, there could be no equality of different functions and no purpose for a good beyond the diversity and

10. Cf. Charles N. R. McCoy, *The Structure of Political Thought,* New York, McGraw-Hill, 1963, Chapters I and II.
11. Norman O. Brown, *Love's Body,* New York, Vintage, 1966, p. 121. Lionel Trilling also delineated the consequences of a similar concept, which he called rather "the democratic pluralism of sexuality," in connection with the Kinsey Report. Cf. *The Liberal Imagination,* Doubleday Anchor.
12. *Ibid.,* p. 225.

no regularity by which any further good could be achieved. The burden of these new concepts is to overturn these natural, hence, political stabilities. "To be awake is to participate, carnally and not in fantasy, in the feast; the great communion . . . . Polymorphous perverse sexuality, in and through every organ of perception." [13] Brown, of course, is correct in clearly realizing that the overturning of the natural sexual distinctions and the morality and politics built on them implies a totally new social world.

In her essay on Brown's other book, *Life Against Death,* Susan Sontag points out that "the revolutionary implications of sexuality in contemporary society are far from being fully understood." [14] The difficulty with psychoanalysis has been that it left the structure of public life intact and sought for corrections in the subconscious, private part of the individual. Brown, taking themes from Freud and, significantly, Christian eschatology, attempted to argue that the real difficulty lay in the external structure of civilization itself, primarily in the ethic and culture built upon the distinction of the sexes which projects the birth and education of the child. The result was that we need now "bodily" changes so that we can really experience the "resurrection of the body" in all its unlimited (that is, no norms) potentialities. "We are nothing but body; all values are bodily values," says Brown. He invites us to accept the androgynous mode of being and the narcissistic mode of self-expression that lie in the body. According to Brown, mankind is unalterably, in the unconscious, in revolt against sexual differentiation and genital organization. The core of human neurosis is man's incapacity to live in the body — to live (that is, to be sexual) and to die." [15] Miss Sontag sees that

13. *Ibid.,* pp. 255, 249.
14. Susan Sontag, "Psychoanalysis and Norman O. Brown's *Life Against Death,*" *Against Interpretation,* New York, Dell-Delta, 1966, p. 257.
15. *Ibid.,* p. 259.

the eschatological concepts relative to the resurrection of the body in this new secular view foreordain the elimination of classical sexuality in the bodily life itself.[16]

The historical meaning of this level of criticism is far-reaching. Herbert Marcuse's *Eros and Civilization* professes to be prophetic of the final overcoming of classical sexuality, rationality, and civilization. The "reality principle," which functions as the justification for controlling man's natural instincts in the name of order and progress, is the real cause of man's discontent with both death and progress, and the real cause of man's discontent with both death and society. All liberation from man's suppression is, in Western thought, merely abstract; it does not touch the real problem.

Western philosophy ends with the idea with which it began. At the beginning and at the end, in Aristotle and in Hegel, the supreme mode of being, the ultimate form of reason and freedom, appears as *nous,* spirit, *Geist.* At the end and at the beginning, the empirical world remains in negativity — the stuff and tools of the Spirit, or of its representatives on earth. In reality, neither remembrance nor absolute knowledge redeems that which was and is.[17]

The real values of man remained locked up in the spirit beyond time, as it were.[18]

For Marcuse, Nietzsche's eternal return at least represents an advance because it strove to save precisely this earth where all suffering and violation had taken place.

Eternity, long since the ultimate consolation of an alienated

16. This too must be seen in the context of the overall relation of this aspect of life to the elimination of the distinction in things themselves. Cf. the author's, "The Significance of Post-Aristotelian Thought in Political Theory," *Cithara,* November 1963.

17. Herbert Marcuse, *Eros and Civilization,* Boston, Beacon, 1966, p. 118.

18. *Ibid.,* p. 121.

existence, has been made into an instrument of repression by its relation to a transcendental world — unreal reward for real suffering. Here, eternity is reclaimed for the fair earth . . . . Death is; it is conquered only if it is followed by the real rebirth of everything that was before death here on earth — not as a mere repetition but as willed and wanted re-creation. The eternal return thus includes the return of suffering, but suffering as a means for more gratification, for the aggrandizement of joy.[19]

Yet, this must become an action program. All the realities of existence, of historic suffering and injustice must find a source of reorganization outside the structures of the present alienated labor of actual civilization.

The only thing that escapes from the reality principle of public political organization is phantasy. This is rooted in man's rejection of civilization's control over the expression of his instinctual desires. He can dream contrary to actual organizational procedures and structures. The only way to overcome the consequences of the rule of the *Geist* or of a projected eternity beyond the grave is to restore to man in his actual bodily reality all the desires and relationships that were suppressed by the reality principle which demanded their control. Phantasy becomes the key to how reality must be reorganized.

"In so far as sexuality is organized and controlled by the reality principle, that is, through so-called normal, monogamous structures, phantasy asserts itself chiefly against normal sexuality," Marcuse writes.

However, the erotic element in phantasy goes beyond the perverted expressions. It arrives at an "erotic reality" where the life instincts would come to rest in fulfillment without repression. This is the ultimate content of the phantasy process

19. *Ibid.,* p. 123.

in its opposition to the reality principle; by virtue of this content, phantasy plays a unique role in the mental dynamic.[20]

What has made sexuality in all its erotic forms reappear again out of mere phantasy is the evolution of industrial society in which the forms of oppression in the name of work and order are no longer necessary. The long-range result of this would mean the destruction of the basic forms of repression caused by the operation of the reality principle. "This change in the value and scope of libidinal relations would lead to a disintegration of the institutions on which the private interpersonal relations have been organized, particularly monogamic and patriarchal family." [21] The repressive, civilizational aspect is upheld by the notion of the genital supremacy which necessarily results in strict control of sex in the name of so-called higher ends. Marcuse argues for a polymorphous sexuality which eroticizes reality so that all relationships can be liberated from the classic forms of restrictive sexuality, that is, the monogamous.[22]

Sexuality grows into eros which is a metaphysical concept describing the nature of non-repressive being.

Under non-repressive conditions (that is, under conditions in which the classic forms of sex, family, and state do not exist) sexuality tends to 'grow into' eros — that is to say, toward self-sublimation in lasting and expanding relations (including work relations) which serve to intensify and enlarge instinctual gratification. Eros strives for 'eternalizing' itself in permanent order.[23]

This, of course, must confront the problem of how death, *thanatos,* is overcome in this new concept of the resurrection of the poly-

20. *Ibid.,* p. 146.
21. *Ibid.,* p. 201.
22. *Ibid.,* pp. 201-11.
23. *Ibid.,* p. 222.

morphous flesh. Marcuse recognizes that time is repression's ally.[24] But he is concerned to redeem the actual sufferings of historical men and will not grant any vicarious or non-real solution.[25] Since he cannot grant the force of the Christian concept of crucifixion and resurrection, that is, a redemption of the real man who actually suffers in this life but who still must die, he must attempt to eliminate death and substitute for it mere pain, especially unjustified pain which, presumably, can now be removed from mankind.[26] The force of society must be then to eliminate this pain by the experience of pleasure in all its aspects. The claim to anything more would be seen as simply improper and therefore, supposedly, unannoying to the sufferer.

There is a sense in which Karl Marx had already foreseen this development and treated it in a more profound manner. For Marx, the forces of the Aristotelian and Hegelian traditions could not so easily be abandoned. Marx saw that the concrete identification of man with his species and his species with all nature, hence all being, would, conceivably, unify all reality under the concrete form of all being that historically had existed. This was to be accomplished by the positive elimination of all alienation, especially natural alienation. This meant that the so-called normalcies of nature had to be positively overcome in order to attest to man's identification of all being with himself.[27]

While Marxist movements themselves have ended up almost by accepting the validity of the original Aristotelian normalcies, the more radical contemporary philosophies are still enamored with Marx's notion that the overcoming of natural sexual forms is the most positive and direct way to discover all being and transform man. Kate Millet's essay, "Sexual Politics: Miller,

24. *Ibid.*, p. 231.
25. *Ibid.*, pp. 236-37.
26. *Ibid.*, p. 235.
27. Cf. Karl Marx, "Economic and Philosophic Manuscripts," T. B. Bottomore, trans., in *Marx's Concept of Man*, E. Fromm, editor, New York, Ungar, 1961, pp. 90-196.

Mailer, and Genet," suggests the further developments of the notion that the heterosexual distinction is precisely what needs to be overturned to eliminate repression in society. In analyzing Henry Miller, Norman Mailer, and Jean Genet, Miss Millet traces the implications of sexuality in forms other than the traditional male and female roles. Love is immediately transformed into power and dominance when the diversity of the sexes no longer has biological and ontological origins.[28] Indeed, even Genet's analysis of homosexuality's artificial creation of parody sexual distinctions must fail:

> Having studied human relationships in the world of pimp and faggot, Genet has come to understand how sexual caste supercedes all other forms of inegalitarianism: racial, political and economic. *The Balcony* demonstrates the futility of all forms of revolution which preserve intact the basic unit of exploitation and oppression, that between the sexes, male and female, or any substitutes for them. Taking the fundamental human connection, that of sexuality, to be the nuclear model of all the more elaborate social constructs growing out of it, Genet perceived that it is itself not only hopelessly tainted but the very prototype of institutional inequality. He is convinced that by dividing humanity into two groups and appointing one to rule over the other by birthright (i.e., Aristotle), the social order has already established and ratified a system of oppression which will underlie and corrupt all other human relationships as well as every area of thought and expression.[29]

28. This in part explains the great pains to which recent writers subject themselves in order to distinguish the experience of sex in all its generic aspects from any natural exploitation that supposedly arises from the deviant behavior itself because of its very nature. Cf. Marcuse, p. 203. Cf. Richard Milner, "Clap Hands for the Orgy," *The Hippie Papers,* J. Hopkins, editor, New York, Signet, 1968, pp. 110-14.

29. Kate Millet, "Sexual Politics: Miller, Mailer, and Genet," *New*

The sexual origin of politics so visible in Aristotle (and also in *Genesis*) in the sense that the family is the foundation of the state are seen, then, by Genet to be the very causes of human exploitation. This, of course, transcends the limits of mere human exploitation for the distinction of the sexes is from nature. In other words, it is the very structure of the universe that is at fault.

This means, therefore, that the very distinction between the sexes must be removed — a conclusion we have seen already in one form of genetic theory, in the elimination of sex itself, or here in Genet, in the elimination of any uniqueness of exclusive heterosexual relationships so that sex is precisely polymorphous.

> The political wisdom implicit in Genet's statement in the play is that unless the ideology of real or fanaticized virility is abandoned, unless the clinging to male superiority as a birth-right is finally foregone, all systems of oppression will continue to function simply by virtue of their logical and emotional mandate in the primary human situation.... In Genet's analysis, it is fundamentally impossible to change society without changing personality, and sexual personality as it has generally existed must undergo the most drastic overhaul.[30]

American Review, No. 7, New York, Signet, 1969, pp. 30-31. Excerpts from *Sexual Politics*, copyright © 1969, 1970 by Kate Millet. Used by permission of Doubleday & Co., Inc. Cf. Lucy Komisar, "The New Feminists," *Saturday Review*, 21 February 1970, pp. 27-30.

30. Millet, pp. 31-32.
It is worth calling attention to some of the elements of Irving Howe's rather devastating critique of Miss Millet's thesis:
"I suspect, however, that what troubles Miss Millet is not merely the injustice of sexual discrimination but the very idea of sexual difference. For all that she is so passionate an advocate of the cause of women, she shows very little warmth of feeling toward actual women and very little awareness of their experience. Freud speaks in his essay on 'Femininity' of the woman's 'active pursuit of a passive function,' and Miss Millet finds the phrase 'somewhat paradoxical,' thereby revealing a rather comic ignorance of essential experiences of her sex, such as the impulse toward the having of children. Indeed, the emotions of women toward children don't exactly form an overwhelming preoccupation in *Sexual*

"Human liberation" and "equality" are thus conditioned upon removing this heterosexual obstacle.

We are nowadays accustomed to think of Sophocles' great figure merely in terms of a famous complex which he himself, at least, never possessed. The result is that we fail to recall that *Oedipus the King* is a tragedy which presupposes that deviation — in this case, incest — and paternal murder are sins that corrupt the civil order. Oedipus' incest and murder, even though not consciously willed by him, are of such a terrific and terrible nature that they overturn the political order which can only retain its unity and authority if the basic sexual relationships — wife-husband, father-son, male-female — are respected. Tiresias says to Oedipus: "The rotting canker in the state is you." [31] His action is a violation of the human norms that support the state. Oedipus himself relates the prophecy: "How mating with my mother I must spawn a progeny to make men shudder: then, be my father's murderer." [32]

Jocasta tried to make Oedipus cease pursuing the knowledge

Politics: there are times when one feels the book was written by a female impersonator. . . .

"Again, one must say, yes of course, there are such instances, just as blacks are still sometimes lynched and often brutalized: but to fail to see the improvement in large areas of black life in America isn't merely political obtuseness of the kind to which the New Left is pledged unto death, it is the snobbism of those who will have nothing to do with the small struggles and little victories of human beings unless these are patterned to their ideologies and slogans. This is the very opposite — in spirit, in feeling, in political consequence — of genuine radicalism. It is, instead, a symptom of the contempt that today rages among our intellectual and professional classes: contempt for ordinary life, contempt for ordinary people, contempt for the unwashed and unenlightened, contempt for the unschooled, contempt for blue-collar workers, contempt for those who find some gratification in family life, contempt for the 'usual.' " Irving Howe, "The Middle-Class Mind of Kate Millet," *Harper's*, December 1970, pp. 124, 128.

31. Sophocles, "Oedipus the King," in *The Oedipus Plays of Sophocles*, P. Roche, trans. New York, Mentor, 1958, p. 36.

32. *Ibid.*, p. 54.

of who he is in the mistaken belief that it is possible to avoid destiny by ignorance. "How can a man have scruples when it is only chance that's king? There's nothing certain, nothing pre-ordained; for it is best to live by chance as best we may. Forget this silly thought of mother-marrying. Why, many men in dreams have married mothers and he lives happiest who makes the least of it." [33] For the Greek tragedian, it is precisely the violation of paternity and sexuality that causes the destruction of the city. The observance of the laws of nature for man are necessary con-ditions and foundations of happiness and order. Man's happiness is, in fact, a limited, mortal one.

Friedrich Heer, in his *Intellectual History of Europe,* has written:

> *monachatus non est pietas* (monasticism is not true piety) is the fundamental thesis of the modern age. The acceptance of the proposition has unleashed the spirit from all bonds. Arbi-trariness, lack of discipline, and base impertinence have char-acterized European thinkers and moulders of the spirit for a long time. They have become impotent. European intellec-tuals cannot rule because they cannot rule themselves. [34]

Max Weber, in the *Protestant Ethic and the Spirit of Capitalism,* made the same point. [35] This means that moderns have forgotten that the search for human perfection needs to be, as the medievals more clearly recognized, circumscribed by humility and religious control if it is to be prevented from destroying the normal life of common man. There is a gradation of perfection which can-not be ignored even for the stability of the social order. The rule of self, however, in its Greek origins, had to do with the

33. *Ibid.,* p. 61.

34. Friedrich Heer, *The Intellectual History of Europe,* J. Steinberg, trans., London, Weidenfeld and Nicolson, 1966, p. 4.

35. Max Weber, *The Protestant Ethic and the Spirit of Capitalism,* New York, Scribner's, 1958, Chapter III.

rule of reason over the passions. It was upon this prior natural rule that the constitutional rule of male over female was based.[36] Most of the classical literary themes of Western thought, those of fidelity, trust, passion, betrayal, hate, were grounded in the ideas that free control was possible for man and that the basic area of this control lay in the relation of man to his own passions and therefore to the sexual life offered to him.

The family, however, was not considered enough to fulfill man so that the great political themes arose precisely to enable man to complete the tasks he had begun in the family. But the state was still for mortals so that the metaphysics of politics did not envision an overcoming of the precise conditions of mortality as such.[37] The Christian contribution to this theory was to grant that the real earthly person's desire for immortality or resurrection was valid, but not to be achieved in this life by political means.[38] This made it possible for politics to be politics and exempt from the unbalancing attack of a political metaphysics which sought to achieve all the attributes of absolute human completeness in this life. As is evident in writers from Marx to Marcuse and the revolutionaries of the contemporary period, the attempt to bring what belongs to the next life into the game of earthly politics is what confuses modern political philosophy.

Leslie Fiedler has continued the suggestions Marcuse made with regard to phantasy. Just as phantasy is the one historic area free from the control of the necessary repressions of society, so its "form," as it were, is found in the arts. The function of modern literature, however, is not, in this approach, to recreate time in its classic sense.[39] This means that the historical experience

36. Cf. McCoy, Chapter II. Cf. also the author's "Spirituality and Politics," *Worldview*, July/August 1970, pp. 12-16.

37. Cf. Arendt, Parts I and II.

38. Cf. the author's "Theory in American Politics," *The Modern Age*, Spring 1960, pp. 150-59; *Redeeming the Time*, New York, Sheed and Ward, 1968, Chapter 6.

39. Leslie Fiedler, "The New Mutants," *Beyond Left and Right*, R. Kostelanetz, editor, New York, Morrow, 1968, p. 235.

of the past and the human values connected with it are no longer of interest. "This development is based in part on the tendency to rapid exhaustion inherent in popular forms; but in part reflects a growing sense of irrelevance of the past and even of the present to 1965." [40] This rejection of the past literature has foreshadowed a new phantasy which seeks out the new forms mankind may take.[41] "More fruitful artistically is the prospect of the radical transformation (under the impact of advanced technology and the transfer of traditional human functions to machines) of *homo sapiens* into something else: the emergence — to use the language of science fiction itself — of 'mutants' among us." [42] There is

40. Fiedler, p. 237.

41. Professor Philip K. Kurland has remarked on this same kind of contrast in the universities:

"The problem of internal politicization is equally taxing on the primary functions of the university as we know it. The objective here is to treat the university as if it were a governmental body which must be democratized to be legitimized. But function of university governance is not power. The function of university governance is the provision of services that make it possible for scholars to research, for teachers to teach, and for students to learn . . . .

The proponents of the new university are riding a tide of egalitarianism that is sweeping before it not only the university but many other institutions . . . . By reducing humans and human activities to statistics, we provide fodder for computers. By reducing humans and human activities to numbers, the new men make them fungible. They are no longer individuals; they are no longer human . . . .

The life of the mind is the focus of the old university. It is only engagement in the rational testing of ideas new and old that justifies the old university's existence . . . . And here lies the essence of the generation gap. For the young have not seen reason put to sleep and more primitive forces unleashed except on an individual basis.

Whether the new university with its preference for instinctual forces over reason, with its preference for egalitarianism over individuality, excellence, and professionalism, with its preference for political rather than intellectual objectives — whether the new university will prevail over the old is not yet fully determined. But the odds are in its favor." Philip K. Kurland, "The New American University," *Vital Speeches,* 1 March 1970, pp. 316-17.

42. Fiedler, *op. cit.,* 237.

to be a new humanism disengaged from "The tradition of human-ism as the West (understand the West to extend from the United States to Russia) has defined it." [43] There is, therefore, a pressure in music and the arts to identify with the most un-orthodox of human types.[44]

But again, as we have noted in Millet, Marcuse, and Sontag, the most radical effort is to attempt to escape from the traditional sexual identifications. "To become new men, these children of the future seem to feel they must not only become more black than white but more female than male." [45] Technology itself has demasculinized the male by placing the radical responsibility for the child's existence on the female. "Earlier, advances in tech-nology had detached the wooing and winning of woman from the begetting of children; and though the invention of the condom had at least left the decision to inhibit fatherhood in the power of the males, its replacement by the 'loop' and the 'pill' has placed paternity at the mercy of the whim of woman." [46] Recent literature, then, has been based on the anti-male, anti-hero concept of sex-uality.[47] It is also, it might be added, more and more anti-child. Certainly, children are becoming less and less important in our communications media.

Traditional maleness, Fiedler continues, is no longer valid. Men seek to retrieve "for themselves the cavalier role once piously and class-consciously surrendered to women; that of being beauti-ful and being loved." [48] Literature, however, cannot and does not present these new ideals in the abstract alone. "Here, at any rate, is where the young lose us in literature as well as life, since

43. *Ibid.*, p. 239.
44. *Ibid.*, pp. 245-46.
45. *Ibid.*, p. 246. For a discussion from a rather opposite point of view, cf. "Woman's Liberation: The War on 'Sexism,'" *Newsweek*, 23 March 1970, p. 43ff.
46. *Ibid.*, p. 246.
47. *Ibid.*
48. *Ibid.*, p. 249.

here they pass into real revolt .... It is finally insanity, then, that the futurists learn to admire and emulate, quite as they learn to pursue vision instead of learning, hallucination rather than logic." [49] In this new world, what Fiedler calls "inner space," there comes about the elevation of ways of life formerly called mad, perverse, or corrupt. These become the norm of progress against the natural and the normal. The moulds of phantasy and literature and art, therefore, are concerned with the real future which can be projected for men.

> In any case, poets and junkies have been suggesting to us that the new world appropriate to the new man of the later twentieth century is to be discovered only by the conquest of inner space: by an adventure of the spirit, an extension of psychic possibility of which the flights into outer space — moon shots and expeditions to Mars — are precisely the unwitting metaphors . . . .[50]

It is this inner space of phantasy, the unlimited and manifold desires unregulated by reason or order of any sort— the metaphysical polymorphous perversion projected upon cultural reality in the form now of action — that constitutes the new political and ontological ethic which purports to defeat time by the experience of all bodily being which now becomes political and philosophical at the same time. Thus, there is to be no distinction between politics and thought, between body and spirit. Needless to point out, this is the very overturning of the classical notions of things belonging to Caesar and things belonging to God.

The "human" in classical thought was fundamentally based upon the belief that man was already something higher than any-

---

49. *Ibid.*, pp. 253-54. Cf. also for the further background of this discussion, Archibald MacLeish's essay, "There Was Something About the Twenties," *The Saturday Review*, 6 May 1967, p. 10ff.

50. *Ibid.*, p. 255.

thing he himself could make or create. This meant that the heterosexual distinction was itself something for the good of man far higher in value and in experience than anything else that might be proposed. It is no accident that the new programs for "equality" which would see in the natural distinctions of men the cause of our present alienations constitute, in fact, a direct dehumanization of man by classical standards. Archibald MacLeish, in a remarkable essay, has put the problem clearly: "For the real issue then is the issue of truth: Is it true — is it *humanly* true — that the old belief in man is gone, and that nothing is left but this shadowy figure flickering in the half light of madness, degradation, and death?" [51]

This "shadowy figure," to be sure, is depicted as the new revolutionary, shadow only in relation to classic standards. Yet, the problem is, as Marcuse rightly suggested, in the order of "eros and thanatos," it is really a question of the resurrection of mortal man. We are told that the alternative to the resurrection of the flesh in a life after death, a life directly related to this life and this cosmos, is rather the total bodily and fleshly experience in a non-repressive concern that eliminates work and rule and avoids all the unjust pain of the human condition. The classic normalcies and their observance are to be seen as nothing more than societal repressions. True revolution, therefore, must destroy sex as it is naturally known in its heterosexual manifestation. But that is the very problem. For the destruction of heterosexuality not only destroys the basis upon which human happiness has been founded, but it also avoids the problem which pain, just or unjust, only conceals. For it is death itself, not just pain that is the problem.[52] The resurrection of human time, whether by memory or anticipation, cannot avoid this eventuality.

The heterosexual distinction is not, in other words, an arbitrary distinction imposed for the dominance of man in this life.

51. MacLeish, p. 13.
52. Cf. Marcuse, p. 233ff.

Rather it is the very condition of man's mortality and of his earthly tasks. This is the profoundest meaning of the revolutionary movements of our time if we study them in their long-range implications. For they themselves, in their deepest metaphysical sense, seek to overturn the rightness of the created distinctions and its consequences in children and population. The incredible challenge that the heterosexual distinction gives to man is that its conservation is the greater humanity.

But heterosexuality itself is a "given." Man need not keep it nor build his society on it. The contemporary tragedy is that the remaining believers in the sanctity of human life and the dignity of man as he is historically evolved are, for the most part, sidetracked and distracted by supposedly humanitarian aspects of birth control and population statistics so that they ignore the implications of these far-reaching themes that threaten to dehumanize man in his very being. For it is nothing less than heterosexuality itself that is now capable of being eradicated, both scientifically and culturally. In the end, it seems right to call this eventuality "madness."

CHRISTIANITY AND HUMAN NUMBERS

The contemporary position of Christianity in regard to human life and human numbers is, seemingly, not unlike that of the classical Niobe, the wife of a king of Thebes, who unwisely boasted over the large number and beauty of her children before Leto, the mother of Apollo and Artemus. In revenge for this apparent slight, the two young gods slew all of Niobe's children before her eyes. Niobe's great grief over the loss of her children finally touched Zeus who turned her into a stone statue. This statue, so the tradition relates, can still be seen to weep in the summertime.

The analogy is clear. For there is to be, evidently, no more praise for prolific mothers of beautiful children by the grim theoreticians of population control. Will the gods, we surely may wonder, be touched again by the weepings for lost children who are no longer to be among us? Will there even be women who want to be mothers? At a recent conservation conference at which angry youth were protesting pollution and overpopulation, an earnest young woman from California proclaimed that "on a planet disfigured and cluttered by humans, the most 'humane thing' she might do would be to bear no children." [1] Is the nobility of this new "secular nun" to be determined, contrary to that of the religious sister, by the fact that children are wrong to have? For the religious woman, children are given up because they are good and beautiful. For the contemporary secular nun, they are given up because they are harming mankind and causing pollution.

Is the Christian view of population, in other words, so overturned by the so-called "facts" that, as many now readily believe, human beings are themselves the threat to mankind? Is all we have left the consolation of tears over children never to receive life? Are the avenging gods to turn in their new wrath and destroy the children who never, as they believe, "should come to birth?" [2] Will the human race only be left with the stone tears of a restricted humanity to remind it of what it might have accomplished had life gone on and grown?

It has been the task of our argument until now to clarify, if possible, just where the real threat to mankind is coming from and what form it is taking. Someone, at least, needs to be shocked

1. "The Angry Voice of Youth," *The San Francisco Chronicle*, 23 September 1970.

2. As an example of the current reverse attitude toward sheer human numbers the following comment is indicative: "He (Larry Barnett, a California State College/Los Angeles sociologist and vice-president of Zero Population Growth, Inc.) believes that the U.S. should have leveled off at 150 million people in 1950. David Brower, a director of the John Muir Institute and a lifelong activist in environmental causes, suggests a total population of about 100 million.. Ehrlich thinks the U.S. could get along nicely on 50 million people." "Holding Down the Population," *Newsweek*, 30 March 1970, p. 35.

and unsettled by what many of mankind's most learned and influential personages are proposing in obscure journals, laboratories, and conferences, proposals that are more and more seeing popular and political light. We should not be surprised that many, in fact, all of these proposals for controlling human numbers are presented under the aegis of human welfare and dignity. But it is ironic too. So long as we continue to ignore the drastic theological, political, genetic, and philosophical overtones of population proposals, so long as we refuse to do the hard thinking that elucidates their long-term implications, we shall certainly be unable to understand or protect the kind of humanity we have been bequeathed by nature and history, the notion upon which the very idea of human dignity is ultimately based.

Jacques Maritain made a remark some twenty years ago which, in the context of what we have been describing, must seem now almost prophetic. "Democracy carries in a fragile vessel," he wrote, "the terrestrial hope, *I would say the biological hope, of humanity*." [3] For, as population discussions begin to clarify themselves ever more clearly in their ultimate and seemingly logical developments, it is the very "biological" structure of man that is the major democratic issue. Whenever we fail to recognize this, whenever we neglect the rational and necessary requirements of man from now on in our human history, it will be no longer merely man's home or his city that will be attacked, but it will be ever more forcefully his very biological form.

However, while it is vital to trace out the logical consequences of proposals of our day, something we have sought to do, still this does not mean that no concrete population problem of any sort exists, even less that we are exempt from thinking about its hard realities within the context of the absolute value structures to which we, as Christians and men, are committed. Many will

3. Jacques Maritain, *Man and the State*, Chicago, University of Chicago Press, 1951, pp. 69-70. Italics added.

object, of course, to still talking about absolute values in this area, at least as applied to men and not to nature. But we, at least, still insist upon it. For it is relatively easy to solve the population problem by changing our ethics.[4] This is, in fact, what is happening. And this is why it represents the great dehumanizing element arising out of this sector of modern thought. Yet, while there can be no longer any doubt about the totalitarian and anti-human elements in a large segment of current population thought, the world still does have, nonetheless, a need to confront the admitted difficulties caused by disproportionate rates of population growth.

Yet, the desirability and need of population objectives is itself something that falls within the realm of human dignity. To state the problem does not, *ipso facto,* justify all conclusions and means selected to confront it. "A population policy designed to reduce fertility," Professor Dennis Wrong has written,

> must be an integral part of development schemes if the gains of higher productivity are not to be used merely to support a larger population whose further growth will eventually wipe out the very achievements in mortality control and improved conditions that have already been won.[5]

There is, however, little doubt — even on practical political grounds — that we need to approach population in a manner that avoids the fantastically anti-human elements in current abortion, sterilization, ecological, and homosexual proposals implicit in most articulate and strident population control circles. To be presented with these as the only alternatives must come close to the nadir of human thought in our time.

4. Cf. Ben Wattenberg, "Overpopulation as a Crisis Issue: The Nonsense Explosion," *The New Republic,* 4 & 11 April 1970, pp. 18-22.

5. Dennis Wrong, *Population and Society,* New York, Random House, 1966, p. 115.

In part, many of these anti-human conclusions are reached from an a priori, metaphysical origin which stands in direct opposition to classical and Christian values. These origins, we have suggested, must be illuminated and isolated before it is too late to save humanity. But in part, too, these dire "practical" population control measures are chosen by many otherwise conscientious and noble people because they find themselves in an apparently blind alley that finds no way out of the dilemma except supposedly through these dire, indeed atrocious alternatives, often enough admitted to be contrary to the classical tradition of human dignity.

The topic of "pollution" — air, water, environment — has in fact suddenly become the theoretical focal point around which most population discussions take place.[6] Earlier (Chapter I), we have discussed the intellectual origins of this phenomenon. Pollution has, indeed, become such an impassioned topic that the very primacy of man on earth is questioned, if not actually rejected. Indeed, it might well be argued that the prophecies of doom associated with religion and chiliastic fanaticism have now been secularized, as it were, and have found a new home among the popularizers of ecology and environmental studies.[7] Like their religious forebears, the great curiosity of such modes of thought is the degree to which they stand outside the human-

6. Cf. Alexander B. Adams, *The Eleventh Hour*, New York, Putnam, 1970; Nicholas Roosevelt, *Conservation: Now or Never*, New York, Dodd, 1970. *Man's Control of the Environment*, Washington, Congressional Quarterly, 1970; Robert Arvill, *Man and Environment*, Pelican, 1969.

7. In what must be a monument of this kind of neo-apocalyptic literature, Paul Ehrlich recently published an essay in *Ramparts* (September 1969) entitled, "The End of the Ocean." The cover of this issue of *Ramparts* shows a tombstone sitting in the middle of a dried ocean bed with dead starfish and scrummy shells all about. On the tombstone is inscribed: "The Oceans, Born, Circa 3,500,000 BC, Died, 1979 AD. The Lord Gave and Man Hath Taken Away, Cursed Be the Name of Man."

How could one possibly improve on this kind of nonsense?

istic origins of Western thought. Some dramatic evil — now defined in scientific rather than spiritual terms — is about to engulf mankind. What this ultimate tragedy exactly will be is as varied and as uncertain as can be imagined.[8]

A recent editorial in *The San Francisco Chronicle* summed up, in a popular way and with some perplexity, the most extreme of these recent prophecies: One group of scientists has warned that carbon dioxide in the atmosphere would heat up the earth and eventually melt the polar ice-caps. This would cause flooding. A second group of scientists predicts on the contrary that the sun's rays will be cut down and cause increased ice formation, perhaps a new ice age. "If, however, this distant vision of doom fails to chill the human heart," the editorial continues,

> Dr. Watt (a Professor at the University of California at Davis testifying before a Congressional Committee) has some less remote intimations of catastrophe that warrant concern. He says that overpopulation has created the air-pollution and is the source of numerous other threats against human life as we know it. He says that the U.S. population is already twice what it should be . . . .
>
> Furthermore, he predicts the countryside will be stripped of its recreation areas and its forests in the effort to provide more acreage suitable for farms and grazing lands.
>
> It is notable that Professor Watts' voice is one in a growing chorus of expert opinion concerning the grave and imminent menace of overpopulation. Regardless of whether it brings on melting ice caps, widespread glaciation, or ordinary starvation,

---

8. The essentially "religious" atmosphere of the population control movements should not be overlooked — their missionary zeal, their prophecies of doom, their absolute certitude about the earthly future, their ceremonial rites. Comparative religionists do us a disfavor to neglect a thorough study of these organizations from the viewpoint of religious sociology and comparative religion.

its potential for deep trouble is obvious. The problem is real and plain to be seen and begs for the prompt attention of national leaders around the world.[9]

This editorial is remarkable in many ways. It seems to ignore logic quite innocently when, noting two contradictory proposals, one for freezing to death and the other for being overheated, it concludes not that both *may* be wrong, but that one *must* be right. Secondly, there is even more of a noticeable failure to understand or refer to the implications of recent technology and the nature of the human spirit itself. And finally, there is little political sense of the political consequences of a United States reduced to half its present population size.[10]

There is a further practical and theoretical difficulty to this popular kind of editorial and scientific thinking. As Glenn T. Seaborg, the Chairman of the U.S. Atomic Energy Commission has written, it also ignores the lessons of nature herself and man's place in it. Nature herself abandons many species and growths during the ages. Nature does not preserve all things that she produces. Most of these species that did disappear, furthermore, disappeared because of lack of ability to adapt. Man must learn to understand and control those things which harm his existence. But he has a brain. He can do this. He can counteract the ways he has harmed his own condition. "We also have, and are

9. "The Human Catastrophe," *The San Francisco Chronicle,* 21 September 1969.

The British journal, *Nature,* as we mentioned in an earlier chapter, is probably the best source which challenges on scientific grounds this dire type of thinking and the supposed facts on which it is based: Cf. "On Which Side Are the Angels?" *Nature,* 27 December 1969, pp. 1241-42; "Commonsense on Environmental Pollution," *Nature,* 10 January 1970, pp. 122-23.

10. One of the reasons for concern about the Third World in population studies is the fact that growing disbalances in population proportions do have serious political consequences. Cf. Nathan Keyfitz, "Privilege and Poverty: Two Worlds on the Same Planet," *The Bulletin of the Atomic Scientists,* March 1966.

further developing, the scientific knowledge and tools to better understand the environment to allow us to forecast the effects of technologies, their trends and social implications, and therefore to have the knowledge to plan ahead to avoid trouble." [11] It is clear, then, that human genius and capacity can improve upon nature in the name of man. Indeed, it must do so. Nature may already have destroyed more plant and animal species than man has yet accomplished. What he must do is to decide on those things that are passing away. Which one does he want to keep. Moreover, man has invented, even in nature, many things which nature could not develop by herself. Practically all animals and plants that we now know are, in one sense, man-made.

Indeed, the basis of the agricultural revolution itself is man's capacity to improve on nature within the structure of the very animal and plant species themselves. Consequently, the ideal of "preserving nature intact" is itself an artificial thing, attempting to stop an on-going evolution which does not always preserve what man feels necessary or beautiful. Such a view of nature can become destructive and dangerous as an ideal in the light of what nature herself actually is. If evolution is true, if it develops toward the hominization of the earth, then any drastic reduction of earthly population or a restriction of the natural environment merely to what "nature" has already produced is itself very illusory and a denial of the evolutionary potentials both of nature and of mankind. Are we forbidden to control volcanoes, their gases and dust, or earthquake effects, or lightning, for example, because nature produces them and thus pollutes the atmosphere and destroys the environment?[12] We are never

11. Glenn T. Seaborg, "On Pollution," Science Service, in *The Los Angeles Times*, 4 May 1969. Cf. Glenn T. Seaborg, "An International Challenge," *Science and Public Affairs*, November 1970, pp. 5-7; "Science Technology, and the Citizen," *Vital Speeches*, 15 October 1969, pp. 5-10. Cf. also Philip M. Hauser, "On Population and Environment," *Vital Speeches*, 1970, pp. 696-701.
12. "In spite of the practical character of many of the reports which

far from the essential question of what the earth is for.

In his recent summary of American proposals to control population, Jonathan Spivak summarized the growing evidence that population size is primarily a function of the deliberately desired number of births per family and not so much of the lack of techniques of control. But since the "desired" number is already too large in the United States (and throughout the world) for what many demographers think to be "sufficient," the result is that we have a growing variety of proposals which seek to reverse this growth trend. The most widely discussed of these already familiar themes are:

---

appeared as working papers at the conference (Countryside, 1970, London), there has been an awkward sense that conservation is next to godliness and that, in any case, the management of the environment needs some central mechanism for keeping the wayward tendencies of ordinary people within bounds. And in spite of the protests of some of the delegates, the conference has been an occasion for resurrecting old concepts such as the view that there is nothing wrong with the environment that would not be cured if people were abolished.

The conference this week seems to have fought shy of the most serious problem of all — the irradicable conflict between the wish of most people to become more prosperous and the likelihood that, if they do so, they will help to damage the environment. This, certainly, is why the solicitude of prosperous populations such as that of the United States for the environment sounds hollow to peoples in developing countries....

Two opposing tendencies are disquieting. There is a risk that conservationists may be found to have embraced unnecessarily authoritarian views of what should be done to preserve the natural environment. Another possibility is that conferences like that at Guildhall this week will have allowed many people to pretend that they are on the side of the angels while caring nothing for the better management of the environment.... Is it not important that jet aircrafts, much reviled, have nevertheless made it possible for thousands of Englishmen to spend their summer holidays on other peoples' less crowded beaches? And is it not important that industrial technology has provided them with the prosperity with which to pay their fare? In the long run, the narrowness of last week's conference will be its undoing next time round. It is to be hoped that the Duke of Edinburgh will not lend his support to the supposed conflict between technology and environment, but rather to the view that both of them can be exploited to everybody's benefit." "Palace and Environment," *Nature,* 31 October 1970, p. 399.

Removal of the tax exemption for children and other modifications in Federal income tax policy to favor the single wage earner at the expense of married couples;

Denial of college educational benefits to children in large families, and imposition of higher property taxes on such families to support the public schools.;

A government ban on early marriages to reduce the span on fertility;

Open approval of homosexuality and other deviant behavior which cannot cause conception;

Encouraging women to continue their education or obtain employment — birth rates, not unexpectedly, are low among PhD's and other working wives;

Perhaps the most Orwellian alternative (is) . . . the addition of a fertility depressing chemical to the water supply . . . .[13]

The implications of these proposals are that nothing short of powerful social and political control will sufficiently curb population growth.

But this is not all. What is even more significant is that the historic rights and duties of man developed so painfully in the long process of Western and world thought must seemingly be abandoned in large part because of this supposed necessity for political control of population. Yet, as Spivak remarked, popular government does have to protect its political base and realizes that such proposals are unlikely to be viable for "population control ultimately involves the ultimate in Government authority — imposing sanctions on the individual's right to reproduce." [14] This imposition would undoubtedly cause "social unrest," to say

13. Jonathan Spivak, "Population: A Whiff of Political Dynamite," *The Wall Street Journal*, 15 September 1969. For an excellent survey of the practical aspects of these and similar proposals, cf. Bernard D. Davis, "Prospects for Genetic Intervention in Man," *Science*, 18 December 1970, pp. 1279-83.

14. Spivak.

the least. What this means is a coming, inherent conflict between the ethical tradition of the people and the control proposals of a messianic elite claiming superior knowledge about the welfare of the people themselves, especially in this fundamental area of reproduction. Indeed, logically, it implies more than this. For it questions the very right of popular government, habitually weak in the face of this question, to exist. Thus, there are more structural and moral overtones to population than we are likely to suspect.

In the light of these almost monotonously authoritarian control proposals, is it possible to discover an approach to population which does not conclude implicitly or explicitly to the necessity of widespread abortion, sterilization, water depressants, deviant life forms, or absolute state control as the only solutions? In one very accurate sense, the degree to which these proposals are widely held today represents the extent to which ethical thought about the absolute dignity of man is evaporating in our civilization, thought, and politics. It can be objected, of course, that unless these drastic means are soon instituted upon a massive scale, there will be no more "familiar" world as we have known it. But that is precisely the difficulty. For not only do these theories to keep the "familiar" world by such means ignore the implications of evolution and base themselves on a very dated technology, but they already radically affront the ethical and philosophical foundations of human society so that the man who survives because of them does so directly at the cost of ethical norms and of actual sacrificed human lives which are denied existence and growth because of a human theory.

Is it necessary, then, simply to accept the supposedly obvious conclusions that classical ethics have values and norms that are cruelly wrong so that it is required to erect a new value-system in which any "prudential" means to birth or population control are always "ethical" because they work to the direct end of limiting or reducing the total of human numbers? This goal of reduction of human numbers becomes, then, the absolute justifying principle of all ethical and political activity.

In seeking to analyze the implications of these questions, the first, and perhaps most important, problem is that of attitude or confidence. This must be emphasized for, in a very real and paradoxical sense, the human race *can* be convinced that it is incapable of meeting the population crisis in time. There is no automatic mechanism to prevent this kind of failure in intelligence and will. To be sure, forced by the unexpected productivity both of agriculture and technology, most professional population theorists who insist on a reduction of world population have been forced to shift their arguments in recent years from the question of "possibility" to that of "time," that is, we cannot achieve our reductionist goals "soon enough," therefore, famines, plagues, and crises. Indeed, the grounds have tended to shift even further because it is no longer really tenable that the human race cannot provide for itself, so that questions of stress and the quality of the natural environment replace those of the quantity of food and clothing and housing.

We must remember, however, that human enterprise and human genius are, at bottom, products of nerve, of belief in man's capacities. In a very fundamental way, they cannot even be expected, in the normal sense of that term. That is, what man can do cannot be "predicted." This means that we probably do not yet know all the inventions and developments that can be and will be which will aid us. But it also means that we cannot act simply on the fact that because we do not know now, *therefore,* nothing will come about to assist man. Hannah Arendt has stated the situation well:

> The new always happens against the overwhelming odds of statistical laws and their probability, which for all practical, everyday purposes amounts to certainty; the new therefore always appears in the guise of a miracle. *The fact that man is capable of actions means that the unexpected can be ex-*

pected from him, that he is able to perform what is infinitely
improbable. And this again is possible only because each
man is unique, so that with each birth something uniquely
new comes into the world.[15]

It is, then, more than anything else, confidence in the capacities
of the human mind and of human birth itself that enables mankind to succeed at all. The terrestrial destiny of man is, for this
reason, always much greater than any given generation of men
can suppose, bound as it is to its own intellectual and technical
levels.

Almost without exception, then, the contemporary thinkers
most passionately involved about population are those convinced that the provision for a full human life for increasing
human numbers is absolutely impossible.[16] There is, as a result,

15. Hannah Arendt, *The Human Condition*, The University of Chicago
Press, 1958, p. 158. Copyright © The University of Chicago Press,
Chicago, Ill., 1958.
"My own view is that many of the really original and important advances in science stem from the work of young men with few colleagues
and limited resources, who have the time to think hard and deeply about
the problems that happen to interest them. It is important to provide full
support following achievements by such men. *I also consider that general
advances in science are largely made by the application of new ideas
and techniques which come unpredictably from unexpected directions
through curiosity-oriented research, rather than from mission conducted
programs.*" Norman Shepherd, "SRC — Politics and Procedures," *Chemistry
in Britain*, 9 September 1970, p. 378.
In this regard, the remark of Carl Djerassi about birth control methods
and their development is of some interest:
"Except for certain biologicals (special vaccines), essentially all modern
drugs were developed by pharmaceutical companies. I know of no case
in which all the work (chemistry, biology, toxicology, formulation, analyti-
cal studies, and clinical studies through phase III) leading to governmental
approval of a drug . . . was performed by a governmental laboratory, a
medical school, or a nonprofit research institute." "Birth Control After
1984," *Science*, 4 September 1970, p. 943.
16. This may explain something, furthermore, of the decline in interest
in pure research and development in the United States in recent years,
in a loss of hope about what man can do. Cf. Myron Tribus, "Applying
Science to Industry: Why America Falls Behind," *U. S. News*, 18 January
1971, pp. 35-36.

a systematic exclusion of any thought or technology or development that might argue to an opposite exclusion. This pessimistic attitude is, as we have emphasized, a choice, governed by an essentially conservative view of man which is at bottom anti-human and anti-scientific. It is, of course, pictured to be the result of a series of necessary facts. But should the predictions and prophecies of the worst sort come to be true, should there eventuate massive social and political failures — and this can happen in the field of population growth — its cause primarily would have to be traced to a tragic failure in the area of choice and confidence, not in the area of necessary facts. We must, consequently, be especially clear on this point. Mankind has the intelligence, wit, and talent to solve the population problems by ethical political and social means if it chooses to do so. It is nothing less than a slander on creation and human intelligence to believe anything else.

Further, as we have often remarked, we are in immediate danger of limiting human potentialities to the levels of the present by overattention to the pessimistic population prophecies.[17]

---

17. "Our spaceship earth first appeared about 5,000 million years ago, the first life appeared at least 3 million years ago, and modern man about 500,000 years ago. Now, if we make informed conjectures about the energy still available in the sun or the probability of natural cosmic accidents, one can with considerable confidence say that before man there still lies 3 million years — so man is half way along his path." Thomas F. Malone, "The Dangers in the Air," *Impact of Science on Society*, #2, 1970, p. 146.

"We are frequently told that Lake Erie is dead — when the total fish catch is rising, not falling. Lake Washington was on its way to becoming as dead as Erie, so it was said, and its reversal is viewed as a great triumph. And it surely was a triumph of political organization. But the polluted lake was great for salmon fishing, and now the water is so pure it has difficulty supporting the salmon. Air pollution is always unpleasant and lengthy inversion can undoubtedly be dangerous — but automatic emissions are controllable and I cannot help but wonder whether the problem is crucial compared to the carnage we suffer on the highways to which we seem to have become innured, with intoxicated youth the most frequent offenders. Bumper stickers decry DDT across the land demanding its

In a sense, there is an effort to idealize the present levels of scientific and technological developments so that we *must* live in the future according to these contemporary norms which are, admittedly, inadequate. Indeed, we must begin to fear that innovations and development designed to incorporate larger populations are now being deliberately undermined in order, consciously or unconsciously, to make a "population crisis" come about. This will be a level and problem in political ethics that we must begin to pay attention to.[18]

---

total ban rather than regulated usage — but the next generation of pesticides have killed or blinded dozens of people this year — and no American is known to have been injured by DDT.... I have no wish to minimize the seriousness of our environmental problems.... But is it not time to stop frightening the American people and instead demand the very large systematic programme necessary to acquire the data which would permit quantitative evaluation of the risks verses the benefits of all these areas where man's intervention has already or may yet degrade the environment? We need to know far more about pesticide usage, food additives, drugs, industrial pesticide, radiation hazards, atmospheric phenomena and the alleged fragility of the ecosystem than we do today if we are to make social judgments and establish public policy." Philip Handler, "Address," *Nature,* 14 November 1970, p. 606.

18. Cf. Wattenberg. Cf. also the further remarks of Professor Handler who is President of the National Academy of Sciences:
"Q. Why is that so dangerous for this country?
A. Chemistry is the basis of a 40-billion-dollar-a-year industry in the United States, and its products are obvious all around us. This industry, like the pharmaceutical industry, is rather different from most science-based industry in that it pays all the costs of its own applied research but no longer does fundamental research. In the '30's it began to rely on the academic world to do the fundamental research while industry itself did the applied research. This was a clear decision made consciously by corporate management. Now such managements are apprehensive about the current declining status of American chemistry.
Our economy no longer rests on our natural resources. It rests on our brains, on application of scientific understanding. If we don't keep going forward, then the rest of the world is going to pass us, as you can see any time you go past a store that sells radios and television sets from Japan.
In a somewhat different sense, our greatest resource is our trained man-

But the major problem is rather one of a static population model about human potential based upon present criteria. *The Wall Street Journal,* a source with a record of judicious responsibility on the population question, in part because it must be alert to the tremendous developmental potential in modern business and agriculture, sometimes itself falls into the familiar dilemma of confusing smallness of numbers with quality of life. Citing President Nixon's population speech and a noted address of Harvard nutritionist Professor Jan Mayer, the *Journal* pointed out that the problem of population, contrary to popular opinion, is not primarily a question of food supply.[19] Food supply, as we have already indicated, can undoubtedly keep pace with population growth. The issue is rather "whether anyone can stand living in such an overcrowded world. In a phrase by now over-

---

power. And the economic loss from disease, the cost to the country for health care, is a serious economic drain to say nothing of the tragic human costs. The only hope we have of reducing this drain, while averting the tragedy, is research. I offer no guarantee, no promise of success. But if we don't make the attempt, disease—man's most ancient enemy—will take its toll."

"Q. Will we be able to take care of all the ecological problems which science has helped to create?

A. It is true that in some, perhaps numerous, cases, we have done ourselves a disservice. By that I mean we failed to regulate some uses of our technology when the warning signals were already there, and we didn't pay enough heed. We do have dirty streams, dirty lakes and harbors which are less than they ought to be. It also is true that what comes out of the tailpipe of an automobile or airplane or the smoke-stack of a power plant isn't very good for us—and the list of such problems is too long.

But my answer to all of that is we can successfully manage almost every one of our major pollution problems using either available technology or new technology we could soon acquire. We just have to be willing to pay the associated costs. I don't find myself truly troubled. The prophets of doom have predominated recently, but they need not be vindicated. We need only put more muscle behind our newly recognized national purpose." From a copyrighted Interview with Dr. Philip Handler, "Science in America," *U.S. News and World Report,* 18 January 1971, pp. 32-3.

19. *The Wall Street Journal,* 23 September 1969.

worked, it is a question of the quality of life." [20] The speed with which new population comes into being is the problem with this analysis. We do not have time, supposedly, to absorb all the new people. Moreover, "the greatest menace in unchecked population is not the material ugliness and physical discomfort. It is the ugliness of spirit that must grow if the lives of people become increasingly intolerable under population pressure." [21]

It is again clear that this type of analysis ignores almost completely the possibilities involved in the thesis that larger numbers of population are necessary and advisable for the more advanced forms of human society.

Because population growth is currently being linked to environmental problems, we can look there first. The Explosionists say people, and industry needed to support people, causes pollution. Ergo: fewer people — less pollution.

On the surface, a reasonable enough statement; certainly, population is one of the variables in the pollution problem. Yet, there is something else to be said. People not only cause pollution, but once you have a substantial number of people, it is only people that can solve pollution. Further, the case can be made that *more people* can more easily and more quickly solve pollution problems than can fewer people.[22]

20. *Ibid.*
21. *Ibid.*
22. Wattenberg, p. 20. Wattenberg continues: "For example, let us assume that $60 billion per year are necessary for national defense. The cost of defense will not necessarily be higher for a nation of three hundred million than for a nation of two hundred million. Yet the tax revenues to the government would be immensely higher, freeing vast sums of tax money to be used for the very expensive programs that are necessary for air, water, and pollution control. Spreading constant defense costs over a large population base provides proportionately greater amounts for non-defense spending. The same sort of equation can be used for the huge, one-time capital costs of research that must go into any effective, long-range anti-pollution program. The costs are roughly the same for 200 or 300 million people — but easier to pay by 300 million." Wattenberg, p. 20.

Further, it assumes that people are closer together or further apart because of numbers and space, whereas it is much more likely that these proximity problems are more especially direct products of modern communications systems, as Marshall McLuhan has indicated.[23] William H. Whyte's book, *The Last Landscape,* is of fundamental importance in this issue:

> We are, in sum, going to operate our metropolitan areas much closer to capacity and with more people living on a given amount of land.
>
> A prescription for disaster, some would say. The literature of planning and conservation — indeed, American literature in general — has a deep anti-urban streak, and the very reason for the city concentration is viewed as its mortal defect. The terms carry their own censure — "insensate concentration," "urban concentration," "urban overgrowth," "urbanoid" — and by epithet they take it as self-evident that people must pay a terrible price for living close together. Lately there has been much talk about experiments with rats that show that when they get crowded they get neurotic, and therefore, by implication, so must human beings. The bias is also evident on the urban plight. The stock shots of bad things always show forms of concentration: telephoto shots of massed rooftops, telephoto shots of cars jammed on a freeway, shots of harried, nervous looking people crowding sidewalks. *None of this is supported with any research on actual human behavior,* which is a pity, for there are some interesting questions to look into. If people do not like being crowded, why do they persist in going where they will be crowded? How much is too much?
>
> But the questions are somewhat beside the point, and of all people we Americans probably have the least reason for

23. Cf. Marshall McLuhan, *Understanding Media: The Extension of Man,* New York, McGraw-Hill, 1964; *The Medium is the Massage,* Bantam, 1967.

fretting about them. Our densities are not high at all. They are low.[24]

Much of the models of criticism, then, have clearly been static ones, embodying present norms and values as the necessary ideals of social policy. This is the kind of neo-conservatism that underlies all current population proposals designed to reduce population.

The fact is, however, that the total technological foundations of society are already so vastly transformed and transfused that we can hardly imagine the size or quality of human population that is possible for man if he does not choose to limit himself to present levels and be content merely to repeat what he has already produced.[25] It is much more likely, ultimately, that the

---

24. From *The Last Landscape*, by William Whyte, pp. 9-10. Copyright © 1968 by William H. Whyte. Reprinted by permission of Doubleday & Co., Inc.

"A lot of nonsense is heard these days about the psychological effects of living too close together in cities, or of living in cities at all for that matter. Many of the stock criticisms are quite ancient — filing-cabinet apartments producing filing-cabinet minds, neuroses, tenseness, conformity, and so on. But now the accusations are being made more scientifically. There is a rash of studies underway designed to uncover the bad consequences of overcrowding. This is all very well as far as it goes, but it only goes in one direction. What about overcrowding? The researchers would be a lot more objective if they paid as much attention to the possible effects on people of relative isolation and lack of propinquity....

If we study the way people themselves live, we will find strong empirical evidence that they can do quite well in high-density areas...." Whyte, pp. 382-83.

25. "There's not one item of modern technology that we've acquired since 1810 that would have been possibly accredited or even dreamt of....

Energies, apparently, are finite and accountable. This law, the law of conservation of energy, states that energy cannot be lost, created, or destroyed. Which is simply to say that the working assumption of the best minds up to the time of the turn of the century, that the universe was running down, is no longer tenable.

This fact, that energy is not lost, has not yet found its way into our books on economics. In them we still find the word "spending" — a word referring to that now outdated thinking before man knew that there was a speed of light...."

problem in the future will be caused by the non-necessity of work
on a gigantic scale, by the practically unlimited availability of
energy, by the possibility of inhabiting the whole globe, and
the quality of life far more complex, advanced, and progressive
than anything we know by projecting merely contemporary
standards and goals.[26]

The history of population control has passed from predominant-
ly moral categories as seen in Malthus and, until recently, in most
Christian thinkers.[27] In the light of the so-called failures of moral

---

I would say, then, that what we probably mean by 'wealth,' really
has something to do with how many forward days we have arranged
for our environment to take care of us and regenerate us in life and give
us increased degrees of freedom.

Now, regeneration of life is produced first with energy, which we
have in two fundamental conditions: energy associative of radiation that
can be focused on the ends of levers, etc.; and energy as radiation that can
be converted into energy as mass or matter, and vice versa. Now we find
that the energy part of the universe is conserved — that it cannot be
created or be destroyed — and we use the energy as matter for levers
and energy as radiation to impinge on the ends of levers. This is really
the fundamental great general scheme. Energy is conserved and there's
plenty of it. Every time we rearrange our environment, we get more
energy and more levers to do more work to take of the regeneration of
more and more of our forward days. These energies are there and they
cannot be spent.

The other element of wealth to be defined is by far the more important.
It is our intellectual capacity to recognize generalized principles that
seem to be operative in the universe and to employ these principles. This
is man's metaphysical capability, which we use to make an experiment
to find out how the lever works and to discover generalized principles.
There are a number of very important irreversibles to be discovered in
our universe. One of them is that every time you make an experiment
you learn more; quite literally, *you cannot learn less.* That's a pretty
interesting fact, isn't it, because it means that the metaphysical factor
in wealth is one that is *always* gaining." R. Buckminster Fuller, "Education
for Comprehensivity," in *Approaching the Benign Environment,* London,
Collier, 1970, pp. 62, 73, 75-76.

26. Cf. Robert Theobald, *The Challenge of Abundance,* Mentor;
Michael Harrington, *The Accidental Century,* Penguin, 1965.

27. Cf. William L. Langer, "Population Growth and Increase in the

means, together with a period in which economic depression was caused rather by underpopulation, great hope and pressure were placed on the medical and technical aspects of population control.[28] This second period, lasting roughly from 1930 until 1965, believed, mistakenly, that the basic reason for rapid population growth has been historically the lack of inexpensive, simple birth control means and simplified information about how to use these means. Stress was placed on the right of private conscience to choose the means it thought best.

During the past few years, however, with ever increased insistence, the theory is now becoming widely accepted that there is an absolute limit of earthly population of from two to five billion people, preferably the lower figure, which requires, whether the people like it or not, a control over the size and conditions of human families.[29] The terms of this problem are now seen in elitist fashion as issues of social and political guidance or dominance. "Morality" is to be determined solely by the ideal of the rigid limitation of human numbers for the benefit of "humanity." And this limitation is almost invariably, as we have observed, based upon a size of population and a quality of life which is rooted and bounded by the present, usually 1960-70 levels of technical and social development.[30] This is, however, a neo-conservatism of

Means of Subsistence," and Thomas McKeown and R. B. Brown, "Demographic Determinants of European Population Growth," in *Readings on Population*, Englewood Cliffs, N. J., Prentice-Hall, 1968, Chapters I and II. Cf. also Cépède, pp. 37-68.

28. Cf. Alfred Sauvy, *La Population*, Paris, Presses Universitaires de France, 1963.

29. Cf. Carlton Ogburn, "Why the Global Income Gap Grows Wider," *Population Bulletin,* 2 June 1970, p. 34.

30. William H. Whyte has noted the anti-city bias of population theory and Fuller its anti-technological and anti-scientific aspects.

The comment of Caryl P. Haskins, the President of the Carnegie Institute, is also worth noting here:

"Why did a truly indigenous Asian scientific revolution never come about? What was the critical missing ingredient? We can never certainly

202 202 *Human Dignity and Human Numbers*

a novel sort, no longer based on the vital principle of the absolute dignity of human individual life, but upon the group or species which is elevated to the primary unit of consideration and social policy. The classical liberties and dignities of man can and must be sacrificed when they come into conflict with the population levels judged to be "ideal" for the generations of the future.

---

know. But it is worth observing that, throughout the whole history of their development, ancient and medieval Chinese science and technology apparently remained essentially pragmatic and utilitarian in their orientation. In sharp contrast, the experience of scientific advance in the West over the past three centuries has underscored again and again a cardinal point. Although a technology of distinction can evolve and can even reach notable heights in a society of wholly pragmatic outlook, a creative science cannot arise, or, if adopted from without, cannot long prosper in such an environment. Only in a cultural climate where the fundamental drives of curiosity and of the love of discovery for its own sake are understood and cultivated can a true science flourish. Paradoxically, it is only when such a science becomes deeply rooted as an element of high culture that a progressively innovative technology can be maintained over long periods, fusing eventually into the close partnership with which we are familiar today. And even when attained, the partnership can never be taken for granted. The maintenance of its health and vigor requires constant attention . . . .

Now of course creativity, in science as elsewhere, is a deeply personal process. A single scientific genius may be more significant to a developing nation than a hundred compatriots of more ordinary endowments. But this truth is all too likely to be unpalatable in a society where science itself is new and unfamiliar. And there are apparently paradoxical corollaries to further complicate understanding and acceptance. *Though individual creativity is so crucial, it is also true that there is some crucial lower limit to the number of creative individuals in the scientific community of a new nation below which it is hard for society to sustain autonomous advance.* Given the statistical sparsity of unusual scientific talent in any population, it is often difficult for a smaller developing nation to accumulate that number, and, given the hazards of 'brain drain,' to maintain it over a sufficient period of time. Then there is a final, and curiously contradictory, hazard. In the absence of a critical 'scientific volume' of this kind, a single powerful genius in a developing country, with all his constructive potential, may yet endanger a balanced development of science if his enthusiasms and commitments unwittingly impose an unwise initial bias." "Science and Policy for a New Decade," *Foreign Affairs*, January 1971, pp. 244, 46. Italics added.

The fundamental basis of any future population theory, however, must base itself upon the fact of growing human potential, upon the centrality of man, and upon the delicate heterosexual nature of human beings and its relation to the child. The basic anti-child spirit of current population movements must be recognized. The great fact of our time — and in this, we are unique — is that it is now possible to develop a population program *not* based upon this heterosexual relationship. Consequently, it is obvious that the normative value of the heterosexual reality must be chosen and reinforced by social and political means, just as the opposite policies are now being propagated by these same means. Without a commitment to keep the human structure as we have received it from nature, it is vain to think that human heterosexuality and its relationship to the human child as its natural result can really last in the light of current genetic and political proposals.

And yet, this all must be seen within the context of the contrary danger of believing that man himself can be saved without a commitment to his own future potential. There is a natural developmental potential within man, connected with his brain and his hands, which itself cannot be ignored if we are to keep man to be man. It is rather this latter danger that is too often missed by the proponents of population stability.[31]

When, moreover, we break the bond between sexuality and the human child, as we are now in a position to do in theory both biologically and politically, when we reduce the fertility aspect of marriage to insignificance, it follows inevitably that hetero-

31. It may be well here to cite several further analyses which positively face the kind of environmental or population problems we have and place them in a more scientific and forward-looking context:

Wallace S. Broccher, "Enough Air," *Environment,* September 1970, pp. 27-31; James O. Evans, "The Soil as a Resource Renovator," *Environmental Science and Technology,* September 1970, pp. 732-35; "Waste Recovery: Big Business in the 70's," *Chemical and Engineering News,* 2 March 1970; B. Fort, "Garbage, A New Natural Resource?" *Science Digest,* December 1970, pp. 23-27.

sexuality itself cannot long survive without its natural origin and purpose. Any careful attention to population literature, furthermore, surely shows that among the theoreticians of population control, sexuality is not in fact surviving. There is something cynical about our contemporary civilization when it calmly tolerates, even promotes, those forms of sexuality that are intrinsically unrelated to children. *For such sex is unimportant sex.* It has absolutely no potential for external visibility so that the political power can afford to ignore it. The belief that the so-called "love" aspect of sex can survive totally independently of any potential basis in reproduction is unwarranted. For "sex" without any foundation in a reproductive environment cannot exclude itself from or justify itself before other biologically impotent life styles or other theories which separate children from love in order to improve genetically our race.[32]

The obvious consequence of denying any connection between sex and reproduction is, finally, that the common man is to be trusted no longer to be responsible for the race and its future children. Children, that is, future population, in this new environment are to be rationed out among privileged groups or nations, or even worse, elite genetic types.[33] They are to be severely

32. The point at issue is the theoretical and practical divorce of sex and reproduction as a norm, not that all sexual activity is ipso facto to result in conception. It is further interesting to reflect that when nature is naturally "contraceptive" in older women and during certain natural periods, there is never a question of need of means, except perhaps to prevent venereal disease. Thus the very question always turns precisely somehow on the issue of sex and reproduction.

33. "Though artificial insemination and techniques of egg implantation have mind-boggling implications for society, man will be called on to make even bigger adjustments in thinking when science usurps man's most sacred institution — motherhood — and makes it the prerogative of the test-tube rather than of the woman. Already science has learned how to husband the miracle of conception outside the test tube." K. Michael Davidson, "And Now: The Evolution Revolution," *AvantGarde,* Jan-Feb. 1969, in *Current* March 1969, p. 5.

"Q. Will it be possible some day to produce exact copies of individuals?

restricted as a possibility for the ordinary man. Indeed, the "ordinary" man's desires to have children are now believed to be the main cause of the problem. We are just beginning to catch wind of elitist theories which declare that the genetic pools of common men are not worth reproducing so that the "burden" of reproduction is to fall on specially chosen "superior" types, or, even more drastically and logically, simply removed from man completely as part of his life. In this context, the very political and visible result of sex, that is, the child, that which makes sexuality socially effective and significant, is to be rendered futile in the name of some supposed higher value. "Sex" can then be granted ad infinitum to the masses of men — provided no children result.

In this climate, we see the norms of classical ethics worked out in almost a deliberate parody of their original meaning. Today, if we might systematize this "ethic," nothing is to be accomplished except in the light of a "higher good" — ecological normalcy based on past and present evolutionary levels, resulting in severely restricted population. This higher good, then, demands control of human numbers. This is to be achieved as rapidly as possible by political and technical means. Sexuality is "evil" only in so

A. Yes. You want to know how? We can do it with frogs today. And if we can do it with frogs today, we'll be able to do it with people if we really want to. This is the way it is done:
You mate male frog A with female frog B and get a fertilized egg. After the egg is fertilized, by microsurgery . . . the cell nucleus is removed and discarded. Now you go to frog C and remove the nucleus of one of its blood cells, which is then put into the fertilized egg. The resulting frog will now grow up into the perfect identical twin of frog C. But if we could learn to make an indefinite number of replicas of the absolutely perfect species of man, should we?
I think that is an absolutely horrendous thought, and I'll have nothing to do with it. There is no one I trust with the power to manage such a program. No man, no committee has the necessary wisdom. And so, I much prefer that we go on sampling the vast variety of the human-gene pool and all the wondrous kinds of people it produces." From a copyrighted Interview with Dr. Philip Handler, "Science in America," *U. S. News and World Report,* 18 January 1971, p. 34.

far as it produces children, especially more than one or at the very most two. Child bearing may be taken away from the function of human sexuality to improve racial and genetic "qualities" when a superior method for achieving this goal is finally perfected because the reality of sex itself does not argue intrinsically to the necessity of the natural arrangement. Any other aspect of "sex" is purely private and insignificant. There is thus an ethical primacy of "earth" over man so that man is restricted morally because he "interferes" with the earth as it has evolved up to now.

Such is, of course, a "parody" ethic because it proposes to achieve the goals of population control by means that are deforming to human dignity itself in their very operation. And it is precisely within the confines of this illusory ethic that the contemporary discussion is most frightening. For there is within its structure no longer a *reason,* no longer either a philosophical, scientific, ethical, or religious reason for preserving man. This is essentially what has been given up in the present context of means and why anything can be done to man to achieve this new goal. This lack of ultimate metaphysical defense for man will not be, indeed, overlooked in the totalitarian proposals for the control of population. For the *only real kind of a defense man has against the totalitarian state is his dignity as something given, something valuable in himself.* And since this is precisely given up in the name of population means, he then finds himself intellectually defenseless.

We must not delude ourselves into believing that the structure of man will remain stable and human unless we have a "reason" for it. And in the case of man, the "reason" for his structure is an absolute given in nature. It is not itself subject to human alteration or even to human justification. For man does not create the reason why he is himself originally constituted to be man.[34]

34. If man in fact is the cause of his own structure, then, of course, there is no intrinsic reason not to change him any way we choose, for in that case it is not necessary or good that his present form be his

Classical metaphysics and ethics understood this when it placed the ends of man beyond political and biological manipulation. We are now at a moment in history when we can see visibly the consequences of the failure of our society to protect the basic structure of man.

Yet, as if to correct itself, classical ethics must be the first to admit that the visible structures of the modern political and social world, especially as it relates to population, are in great part the results of moral and ethical failures on the part of men and nations. It would be absurd if the effort to defend and maintain the heterosexual ideal and reality in man were understood to mean merely a sanctification of the often dire conditions of human birth and growth today, conditions which sometimes cannot be called ethical by any standard. It is quite legitimate and necessary to emphasize that population pressure is the result largely of deviation from, not conformity to the standards of classical values and ethics.

Indeed, the great danger of the present turn of population thought toward enforcement of technical and medical means controlled by an elite in the name of the masses is that it represents a deliberate abandonment of moral possibility in man as a meaningful alternative to coercion. There is a sense in which the refusal to grant the ethical norms and free responsibility of ethical man can only result in a condition in which he is controlled "for his own good." This becomes the logical consequence once the hope of self or moral control is believed to be impossible of achievement.

The difference between these various attitudes which disagree on the problem of means lies in their attitude toward human failure and on what can be done to prevent it. In fact, classical ethics is much more severe in its strictures against failures in responsibility toward children, their begetting and growth, than

---

best form. Cf. Arendt, p. 137ff.; Charles N. R. McCoy, *The Structure of Political Thought*, New York, McGraw-Hill, 1963.

anything the population control theories of modern times have come up with. But classical ethics, following its metaphysical foundations, allows space, as it were, for human weakness and sin. Hence, these deformities must be allowed to "happen," to work their way out into reality to see their effect. Further, contemporary population theory defines the child, the end-product of failure, as evil; while classical ethics never allowed us to maintain that the child, no matter how begotten, is itself evil merely by being a child. It is the ethical action of the begettors that is the problem, not the result, the child. This sphere of ethical freedom, however, is no longer seen to be legitimate by the newer population ethics. Hence, it is necessary to eliminate the very sphere in which the newly defined evil can happen. There can be no more failures. And therefore, though we are not often made aware of this, no more freedom. What is begotten is itself the evil in this view. No longer is society required to protect and cherish what is real simply because it is human.

Christianity cannot take an indifferent view either to the physical condition of this planet or to the form and dignity of man. Its essential message is based upon the central belief that man as we know him is the greater gift. Further, it is committed to the belief that the world is for man, that human intellectual power is vastly more powerful than we are willing to grant, that it has all the talent it needs to confront this problem within the context of the human. But Christianity also recognizes, perhaps more than most philosophic or religious traditions, that man is a tenuous creature, that it is possible to destroy the very fabric of the human by giving up norms and values that support its essential structure. This can result also from having "too many people," to be sure, but it is far more likely, contrary to recent opinion, that the opposite will be the case. Human dignity is already being undermined by a failure of nerve, a failure to protect and understand the basic essentials of man while seeking to control his numbers.

Human dignity is directly related to human numbers. Mankind does have a destiny that somehow constantly impinges upon his reluctance to accept what he can be in the world.[35] Indeed, we seem to be witnessing, on this issue, the first glimmerings of a rejection by man of his evolutionary destiny. For, in a very real sense, human dignity is itself made possible by human numbers since the quality and complexity of the social, political, and even cosmic life open to man does depend on a large enough number of men to bear the social cost and burden of the potential possible for man. Our major long-range danger today — in spite of the population fear — lies in restricting, not in overestimating this potential.[36]

Human dignity is also, however, the norm of human numbers. A qualitative factor no doubt must influence our decisions about human population. The essential point of this qualitative decision

35. Cf. Colin Clark, "Do Freedom and Population Grow Together?" *Fortune,* December 1960.

It is important to note also the degree to which population discussions currently are studiously avoiding any further analysis of "evolution" as a cosmic prod or destiny or necessity to a further development of man beyond the expectations or even conceptions of the present. This change in the intellectual environment of our times deserves a good deal of study.

36. "From Thomas Jefferson to William Jennings Bryan, American agrarian populists had a dream: a continent populated from ocean to ocean by prosperous farmers, each on his own acres. The prophets of manifest destiny, though far from agrarian, shared the assumption: that the way to conquer North America was to populate it.

The dream is dead. Since the official closing of the frontier in 1900, the population of the U. S. has increased four-fold. Yet the country never really 'filled up.' As anyone who has travelled from coast to coast can testify, the emptiness in places is almost frightening. Even domesticated New England has more wilderness and woodland today than it had at the turn of the century. As a matter of fact the high point for lived-on land in the nation as a whole was 1920.

The trend has been the other way since. Increasingly, the population has been concentrated on a fraction — perhaps one-tenth — of the nation's land area ...." "The Evolution of a Super-Urban Nation," *Business Week,* 17 October 1970, p. 76.

deals with the protection of the human biological and physical heritage. Everyone, of course, would, on the surface, agree with this. No theory sets out to destroy man. But there are choices and practices that undermine and destroy man's basic heterosexual structure. These, it seems, are unquestionably the greater danger. These are being ignored, almost systematically. It is not necessary, nor is it moral, to propose a population control theory that jeopardizes this fundamental element of man. This is what is being done. And this is why population theory contains, in many of its tendencies, so much danger to mankind, even beyond the problem of an adequate life for greater numbers of men.

Human dignity must always be approached from the side of the preservation and development of man. This means, in essence, that for every proposal that is brought forth to determine the numbers and quality of human life, there must be a test, a test of the human. It also means — and this is a philosophic and religious attitude about the nature of man in the universe — that for every proposal designed to control population that does *not* protect the human, there is always another possibility, another order of society, another technique, another innovation so that man is never wholly in the supposed situation in which he has no long-range alternative which can work toward the preservation of man without jeopardizing his basic reality.[37]

37. "In some manner, then, we must chart a course between modern pantheism and denial of unique human rights on the one hand and a latent arrogance toward nature associated with the Christian tradition on the other. Much more important than furnishing statistics on the "green revolution" is to lay the groundwork for an encyclical that would do for the Era of Ecology what Leo XIII's *Rerum Novarum* once did for the Industrial Age." Robert L. Schueler, "Ecology — The New Religion," *America,* 21 March 1970, p. 295.

Schueler accepts the Lynn White thesis about the relation of religion to environment. What is more needed, however, is a much vaster vision of the relation of man to his evolutionary and Christian destiny, a wide ranging reaffirmation of the centrality of man and the function of nature in man's destiny.

No doubt it is true that, for the immediate future, population control methods that violate human dignity — that is, abortion, sterilization, homosexuality, coercion, denial of the rights to bear children — will continue. Nor is there any reason to forbid government — since this is the institution that must deal with men as they are — from controlling such methods in some rational fashion as long as widespread ethical practices tolerate them in fact. What needs to be recognized is that alternative methods are possible provided mankind is willing to develop them. Invention and discovery today are not things that only happen.[38] They are designed also to happen as a result of choice and effort and intelligence. There are moral things yet to be discovered in the social and technological orders.[39] Such is the challenge that human numbers present to human genius and dignity.

In conclusion, this discussion of population problems has concentrated mainly upon the negative and anti-human element implicit in contemporary theories, upon those aspects which seem, more than anything else, to result in a threat to mankind. This stress has seemed necessary primarily because this darker area — the logical connection between population theories and the destruction of the human — is almost totally neglected in contemporary thought. No longer can we afford, it seems evident, to consider these worries to be merely the prejudices and collected biases of Christians when in fact they are the undermining of human values and dignities as such. Everyone, whether he likes it or not, is affected.

In addition, we have stressed also the vast contradictions between the claims of population control theorists and the technological and scientific analyses with regard to the human and natural potential of the earth. This comparison, more than any-

38. Cf. footnotes #15, 25, 30 of this Chapter.
39. It is in this sense that old and traditional things which define historical man come to find newer and fuller realizations as mankind grows.

thing else, has revealed such contradictions and uncertainties that we must consider population fears to be decidedly one-sided in their current public presentations. Such contradictions, furthermore, seem to suggest that the very possibility of man in realizing a more abundant future is conditioned upon a recognition that man needs to remain what he is and that a radical growth in human population may well be necessary if man is to achieve the well-being and evolutionary advance that are historically open to him.

Yet, this is not to deny the drastically unfortunate conditions that exist in many places today. Nor is it to approve any type of population growth as being acceptable for the reason merely that it is growth. Even less is it to suppose that an "infinite" number of men on earth are possible. We have no wish to argue about mathematical theory. It is only to suggest that our present norms are much too narrow even in the light of what we already know and project. In so far as population studies have shown the disproportionate rates of growth and unsatisfying human conditions of many men in the world, they have been of necessary service. They have belatedly forced our attention towards essentially unethical religious cultural, economic, and political patterns causing population and human difficulties. Where the problem with the current state of the discussion lies — and it is, to repeat, essentially an intellectual and historical issue — is in the quality of the analysis about the origins of the difficulty and in the assumptions about what we can do to man's condition in order to solve it.

The world population problem is fundamentally a transitional one, as Buckminster Fuller and John McHale have argued.[40] It

40. Cf. John McHale, *The Future of the Future,* New York, George Braziller, 1969; R. Buckminster Fuller, *Ideas and Integrities,* R. W. Marks, ed., New York, Collier, 1963; *Utopia or Oblivion: The Prospects for Humanity,* New York, Bantam, 1969; *Approaching the Benign Environment,* London, Collier, 1970.

involves agricultural and nutritional developments as well as vast scientific, technical, and political inventiveness. Further, changes in social and cultural patterns that affect needed growth must be made. A methodology of conception regulation that leaves to the human couple practical responsibility over their potential children is in great need. Yet, it must be one that does not, in its intellectual roots, threaten human life or sexuality itself. It should be stressed that present means in this area are, in fact, more or less unacceptable to everyone.[41] This situation will not last in view of the vast efforts being made to come up with a solution that is at the same time natural and acceptable. Nonetheless, in the long run, we do not lack ethical and scientific means to confront the basic problem. We do not lack the capacity to develop what we have already begun — the task, that is, to rethink continually the vast potential of man as he confronts the earth.

We do not even lack, moreover, a firm commitment to man, but rather we lack too often a solid insight into the conditions that threaten his structure. The connection between means of population control and the dignity of man upon which the quality and quantity of human life depend is a very intimate one. It is being ignored and neglected. We must realize that man is a frail and problematic creature, yet, paradoxically, also one with vast potential. He has been given the mysterious gift of freedom according to which he is asked whether he wants to remain himself or whether he really does wish to choose another structure of human fertility and sexuality that is alien to the natural processes which he has been given. Such is the fundamental metaphysical and theological significance of the population question.

The tears of Niobe, the weeping for children who are no longer, children eradicated in wrath because they were so many

---

41. Cf. the author's "Christian Political Approaches to Population Problems," *World Justice*, #3, 1967, pp. 301-23. Cf. also François Russo, "La Terre Trop Peuplée?," *Études,* Janvier, 1971, pp. 49-57.

and so beautiful — this is the serious and poignant condition we are being confronted with. Is it to be a world in which brothers can no longer have brothers, sisters without sisters, even parents without children and children without parents? These are no longer the mere fantastic dreams of the science fiction writers but the concrete proposals of the population and genetic control theorists. This is, philosophically, the result of failing to see the vital connection between the human child and human sexual love. And yet, it is not necessary to jeopardize man to handle the problem of human numbers. What we endeavor to establish, in the end, is that if man is radically deformed because of his reaction to population pressures and theories, it will be his own decision. It will be because he has failed to understand what he is, failed to recognize that what he is is precisely the greater gift, the ultimate reality he must protect and cherish.

AUTHOR INDEX

SUBJECT INDEX